QUILTS BY THE SLICE

QUILTS
BY THE SLICE
SECOND EDITION

BECKIE OLSON

Chilton Book Company
Radnor, Pennsylvania

Published in Radnor, Pennsylvania 19089, by Chilton Book Company

Designed by Anthony Jacobson

Photographs by Tim Scott, Catherine Permin, and Mary Cathcart

Illustrations by Vickie Brann

Color photographs (except last color page) taken at Valley Forge National
Historical Park, Valley Forge, Pa., by permission of the National Park Service,
U.S. Department of the Interior.

Manufactured in the United States of America

Library of Congress Cataloging in Publication Data

Olson, Beckie.
    Quilts by the slice / Beckie Olson. — 2nd ed.
      p.   cm. — (Contemporary quilting)
    Includes index.
    ISBN 0-8019-8131-X (pbk.)
    1. Patchwork—Patterns. 2. Patchwork quilts. 3. Machine sewing.
  I. Title. II. Series.
  TT835.004   1992
  746.9′7—dc20   91-58293
                                                    CIP

1 2 3 3 4 5 6 7 8 9 0   1 0 9 8 7 6 5 4 3 2

OTHER BOOKS
AVAILABLE FROM CHILTON
Robbie Fanning, Series Editor

Contents

Foreword

Remember Uncle Scrooge in the comics? He was most happy diving in his piles of money. That's the way those of us who make quilts feel: we're happiest before, during, and under them.

Beckie Olson's book especially improves the before stage of quiltmaking. To begin with, you, too, will be inspired by the quilts. As I read the book, I found myself wanting to make each quilt.

"Ah, Log Cabin!" I think. "I'll run up a little Log Cabin this weekend." Then I read another chapter. "Churn Dash! I've always loved Churn Dash. Look how easy she's made it."

And that is the allure of Beckie's method. She has figured out the yardages, tested the slicing, done all the trial runs for you. Her methods are fast and efficient and give you another fabulous reason to buy more fabric.

Yet these are not just oversized quilt pieces quickly sewn together. Many have intricate pieces, accurately fitted. The advanced quilts are a delightful surprise. (Who would have thought to slice Little Red School House?) Because Beckie has so much experience teaching in her store, she has much practical information to share: why you shouldn't tear on the crossgrain, why you shouldn't piece borders from crossgrain strips, how to press seams (not automatically toward dark).

But best of all, you'll be able to dive happily into your own pile of quilts.

Robbie Fanning
Series Editor
Creative Machine Arts

Preface

My first quilt was a sorry piece of work. Pregnant at the time, I wanted to make a baby quilt. I chose a hexagon Flower Garden pattern out of a magazine and cut a template out of a piece of cardboard. Luckily I had good sewing skills, so the top really wasn't as bad as it could have been, but the polyester-blend fabric I used certainly didn't help. The quilting stitches were about $\frac{3}{4}''$ long. I won't even talk about the binding. The good that came from that experience was that I loved doing it. I bought a book and decided to try again.

My second quilt was a six-block Ohio Star quilt-as-you-go, which I gave to my mother. It rates right up with the clay ash trays I made at Brownie camp. After that second project I knew I would be a "quilter," but I also knew I needed help.

At that time I was blessed to have as a good friend a talented quilter, Kerry Dunn, who helped me find a host of creative teachers and lecturers. Also at that time my husband, Jim, finished his Ph.D. and accepted a position at the University of Kentucky. Three years later I opened a quilt shop in Lexington. What did I get myself into?

One of the people whose work I relied on the most in those early years as a quilter, shop owner, and teacher was Cheryl Bradkin. Her methods for Seminole piecing formed the foundation for my slicing. The process of cutting, sewing, slicing, and sewing again made so much sense to me.

Barbara Johannah's discovery of quick piecing a triangle was revolutionary in the late seventies. With all the new techniques for triangles, I still go back to this method as the best for me.

Patchwork has to start with an accurate pattern. I learned the skills for making patterns in a class taught by Glendora Hudson in Berkeley, California.

I taught slice classes for five years before I had time to write the first edition of *Quilts by the Slice*, which I have been using now for three years in my classes. I hope my quilting experience and techniques will help you in your quiltmaking.

Beckie Olson
Paradise, Utah

QUILTS BY THE SLICE

Introduction

I started my "affair" with quilts by the slice several years ago with a Log Cabin quilt. I had my fabric stash and a new rotary cutter. I had always been attracted to traditional quilts and quilt patterns, but I was also excited about the newer, quick techniques for constructing them.

There are several methods available for making a Log Cabin. Because I had already had all the "quilt as you go" method I could handle, I quickly eliminated that method from consideration. Piecing by hand was also out of the question. I had also constructed a few Log Cabin projects by cutting out all the small pieces and machine-stitching them together. Not only was it too time-consuming, but I found it difficult to maintain accuracy.

The "strip" methods made the most sense, but there were still problems. First, my instructions said to tear fabric into 2½" strips. I find pieces less than ¼ yard stretch too much when torn. Second, the fabric requirements given in my instructions did not allow for enough extra to straighten the grain of fabric when slicing on the crossgrain. If the fabric was cut, rather than torn, at the store, 2 to 6 inches could be lost. Also, slicing on the crossgrain necessitates piecing the borders. Third, the instructions did not call for ironing as the piecing progressed, which made it difficult to keep the block square. Also, they suggested polyester-blend fabric, which can result in puckering and other problems.

Thus I set out to improve the Log Cabin method. After several months of teaching and improving my Log Cabin by the slice technique, I applied it to several other designs, including Single and Double Irish Chain, Rail Fence, Amish Roman Stripe, and Reed's Rags.

By 1982 I had opened a quilt shop here in Kentucky. The Quilts by the Slice classes were becoming more popular. All the time I was searching for other patterns that could be adapted for slicing. I added a Star Sampler (now Barbara Fritchie Star), Churn Dash, and Jacob's Ladder, all of which have half-square triangles.

Little Red School House was the next Quilt by the Slice. It is not a beginners' project. Although the blocks can be finished in 8 hours, the sashing and borders require extra time. The School House is a grand quilt.

My work on Trip around the World came as a result of a trip my quilt group took to Decatur, Illinois, for the National Quilt Association Show in 1986. While there, we saw a display promoting a book for Trip around the World quilts. We bought the book and headed for home. One woman, who had planned to make a quilt top over the weekend with her sister-in-law, became confused, changed her mind about making a Trip around the World, and instead made a Single Irish Chain. Another woman in the group, after studying the book, didn't make it either. Still another friend lost interest and didn't make an attempt.

Then it was my turn. There had to be a less confusing way. Within two weeks I had developed a different approach and had two quilt tops under way using my Quilts by the Slice methods.

Quilts by the Slice are not just quick quilts made with oversized pieces, but have intricate pieces, accurately sewn together. The quilts in this book all lend themselves to quick machine piecing. I have included several sizes for each design (pattern). Many of the twin-size quilt tops can be completed in 8 to 10 hours. You may not be able to sit for a full 8 hours, but it's nice to know that you can if necessary.

This book is written as if you are taking a class. In the first section of each pattern, you will find the necessary yardage and measurements. All of the questions of how much, how big, and how many times will be answered. Read the complete instructions before beginning. You will find the easier patterns in Chapters 2 through 5. If you are a new quilter, begin with one of these.

I have included in Chapter 1 a list of supplies and equipment that I find helpful for piecing and completing your Quilts by the Slice. Our grandmothers made beautiful quilts with very basic supplies—fabric, needles, thread, and scissors. The supplies available today make the task easier and more accurate. I will tell you why a specific item is suggested, then you can choose.

Chapter 1

Before You Begin

Each chapter following this one contains all the information you need to complete a quilt top in one pattern. I hope, however, that you will take the time to read this chapter as well. Here you will find my advice on the basics—fabric, grain, cutting, pressing, and more. Next, I list the supplies you will need for piecing the quilts in this book.

There are many "correct" ways to make a quilt. I am opinionated enough to think my way is best. The best way for you may be to blend my methods with others. I suggest you give my methods a try as you work your way through these patterns.

The Basics

Fabric—Wash, dry, and iron your fabric so your quilt will be washable. Fold fabric by matching selvages at the top and bottom (Fig. 1-1). If you have selvage only at the top or the bottom, you will be cutting two strips at one time. I do not recommend that. You want to have about a 17″ × 45″ piece after it's folded so that you can cover the folded fabric with your ruler as you slice your strips (Fig. 1-2).

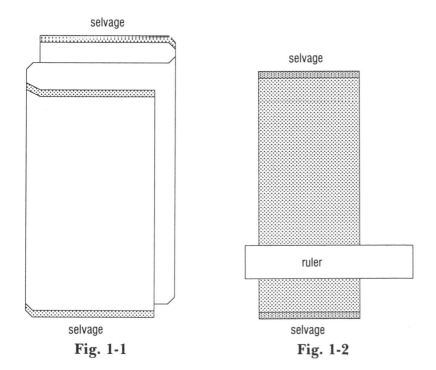

Fig. 1-1   **Fig. 1-2**

The fabric amounts given throughout this book are ample to complete your project, including binding. Draw a fabric cutting diagram before you start cutting—it can simplify your life so much. Figure 1-3 is a diagram for the dark fabric for a twin-size Churn Dash, for example (Chapter 10).

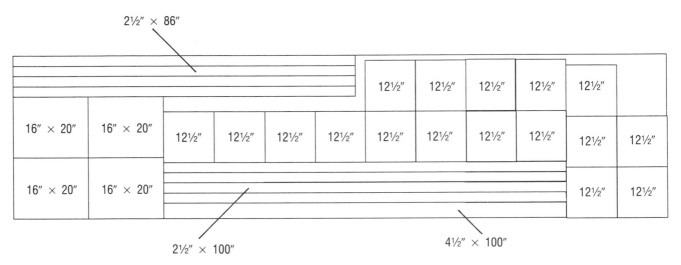

Fig. 1-3

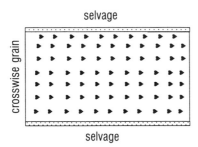

Fig. 1-4

Grain—The grain of the fabric is so important in a quilt. The lengthwise grain is woven more tightly than the crosswise grain, even in good-quality cotton. When slicing, you must consider the pattern as well as the grain. If you are using a regular little print like hearts, dots, or paw prints, it will more than likely run straight on the length and crooked on the width. Thus if you cut the grain straight on the width, it will look as if you did not (Fig. 1-4).

It is more difficult to keep the grain straight when you cut on the width, especially if you folded your fabric incorrectly. If you find your pieces are not on the straight of grain, you can straighten your fabric and cut again, but you constantly have to check each strip. That rarely happens when you cut on the lengthwise grain. Still, I check about every five slices. To straighten the grain of your fabric, make a ¼″ cut on the edge and tear. Refold your fabric, matching the torn edges as if they were selvages. Then cut your next strip ¼″ wider, turn it around, and slice off the torn edge.

Grain is also important during sewing. Some sewing machines feed the bottom fabric faster than the top fabric. This problem is accentuated if the strip is cut on the crosswise grain. I always cut on the lengthwise grain if I have at least ¼ yard. If you are slicing on the widthwise grain because you have a small piece, straighten the grain.

This will make it easier to cut and to sew, and it will stretch less when pressed.

Slicing—The fabric must be folded straight and have no wrinkles in the fold. Lay it on the mat (see Rotary cutter and mat on page 14). The slice you are cutting will be near you, with the bulk of the fabric away from you. Cut your first slice ¼" wider than the directions require, turn it over, and cut the selvage off. Check to see if it is straight. If not, refold and straighten fabric, or tear a ¼" piece off the length of fabric to straighten it (see Grain on page 4).

Sewing—Your stitch length should be 2.5 or about 12–15 stitches to the inch. Check tension and needles, and clean out lint before you begin. Wind a couple of bobbins. There will be little, if any, backstitching.

Seams—For all designs in this book you will use ¼" seam allowance. Check it frequently. See Seam guide, p. 15.

Pressing—Specific pressing information is given for each project. You cannot automatically press the seam toward the dark fabric. One consideration is the direction the piece wants to go; another is how and where you plan to quilt. The intersecting seams need to be pressed so they are going in opposite directions.

You will press on the right side of fabric with a dry iron. Run the tip of the iron along the seam (Fig. 1-5). You can't have extra fabric folded in the seam. Bernette Pro Glide iron, which has a pointed tip and is hot and heavy, is perfect.

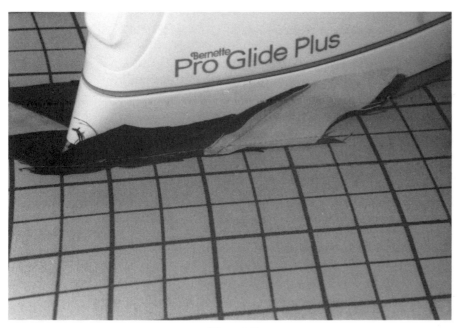

Fig. 1-5

Cutting—When cutting apart blocks that have been sewn onto a strip of fabric, you must have sharp scissors to keep the fabric from slipping. Fold two blocks together, back to back. Make sure the blocks are even, then cut the strip. You can also lay the strip on the table, blocks up, and cut them apart (Fig. 1-6).

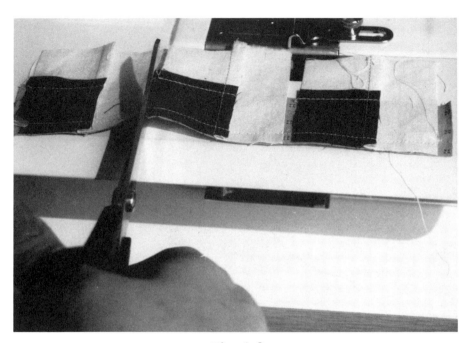

Fig. 1-6

Triangles—You will use Barbara Johannah's method for quick pieced triangles. The triangles are accurate because you will sew on the bias before cutting the yardage, which will eliminate stretching. First, determine the size of the base of the triangle, for example, 2″, and the grid (2⅞″). In this book, the grid size will always be ⅞″ longer than the base of the triangle. Look for the grid size and number of triangles under the specific pattern. Draw the grid on a sheet of graph paper, 8 squares to the inch (Fig. 1-7). Lay the light fabric right side down on the grid (you can tape it in place). Transfer grid lines to the wrong side of the fabric with a long straightedge (Fig. 1-8). It really helps to have the fabric starched for this process. Draw a diagonal line through the squares and then a ¼″ seam line on either

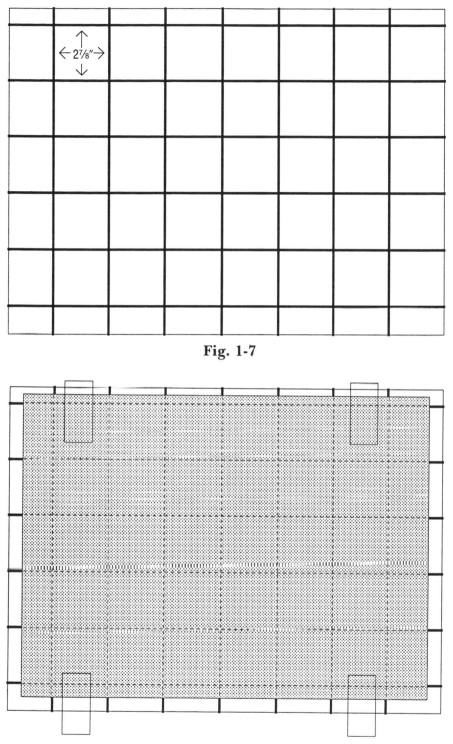

Fig. 1-7

Fig. 1-8

side of the diagonal (Fig. 1-9). The ¼″ seam is very important here. When Barbara Johannah first came out with her *Quick Quiltmaking Handbook* in 1979, she used a ½″ seam allowance. The ¼″ takes so much less fabric and less time (no extra trimming) and is easier to quilt. Pin light fabric (with line drawn) to dark fabric, right sides together. Sew on seam lines starting at one corner (see numbering in Fig. 1-9). Cut apart on horizontal, vertical, and diagonal lines. Press toward dark (Fig. 1-10). Occasionally I see instructions to sew the triangles in a zigzag pattern (Fig. 1-11), but your sewing machine may twist the grain of your fabric when you sew in different directions. The benefit to the zigzag method is the ability to use a directional fabric and have a right- and left-hand triangle. I would rather

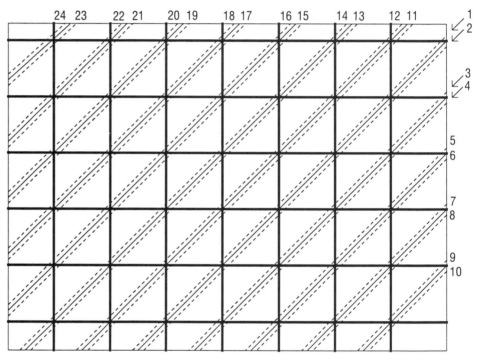

Fig. 1-9

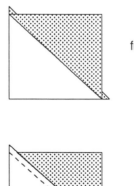

front

back

Fig. 1-10

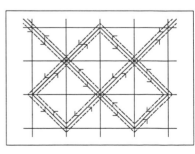

Fig. 1-11

see you change the direction of a whole panel if you are using a print with directional design.

Pinning—Very little pinning is required for projects in this book. You will pin blocks together for placement in the Log Cabin, as well as using the stab-through pinning method on the Little Red School House and the Mormor's Quilt. You will also pin while basting. Pinning can give you a false sense of security while sewing, which can result in slipping.

Borders—The first step is to measure the quilt top *through the center* on the length. I cannot say this enough. It is so important to measure the center of your work. The measurement at the edge might be slightly different due to the seams opening or stretching. The borders need to fit the top.

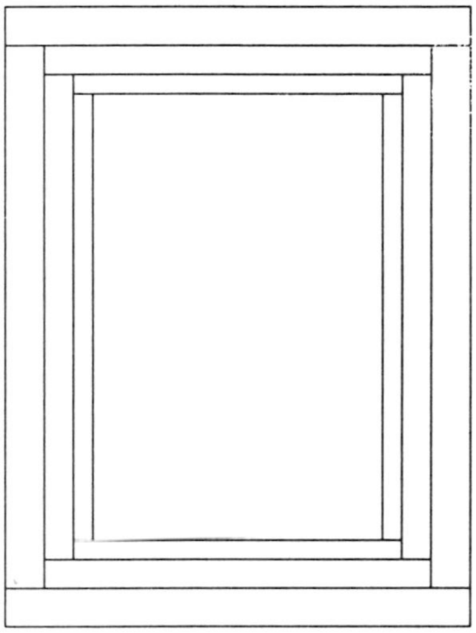

I have used three types of borders for the quilts included in the following chapters. The most commonly used border has what I call Log Cabin corners. The corners of the border look like part of a Log Cabin block (Fig. 1-12). I always sew the long sides first, press the borders away from the quilt, square up the corners, then sew on the top and bottom pieces. I repeat that process for each border that I add.

The second type of border treatment is a mitered border. This is a border with a 45-degree seam in the corner. It starts the same way: first measure the top through the center, on the length and width. The first layer of the border needs to be that length plus twice its own width before sewing plus an inch for safety. For example, let's say that my Reed's Rags top before border is $50\frac{1}{2}''$ wide and $77\frac{1}{2}''$ long. My borders will be finished at $2''$, $3''$ and $4''$. For the first border you need to cut two pieces $2\frac{1}{2}'' \times 56\frac{1}{2}''$ for the width and two pieces $2\frac{1}{2}'' \times 83\frac{1}{2}''$ for the length. For the middle border you need two pieces $3\frac{1}{2}'' \times 64\frac{1}{2}''$ and two pieces $3\frac{1}{2}'' \times 91\frac{1}{2}''$. The last border would be two pieces $4\frac{1}{2} \times 74\frac{1}{2}''$ and two pieces $4\frac{1}{2}'' \times 74\frac{1}{2}''$ and two pieces $4\frac{1}{2}'' \times 101\frac{1}{2}''$.

For safety, these pieces are a little longer than you need. It is easier to trim the excess when you are finished than it is to glue on a little where it is too short.

Before sewing your borders to the quilt, you will first sew the border strips for each side to each other with $\frac{1}{4}''$ seams. Find the center of the length of each strip and, matching the centers, sew them together (Fig. 1-13). Your ends will be staggered. Sew the borders to the quilt top, matching the center of the top to the center

Fig. 1-12

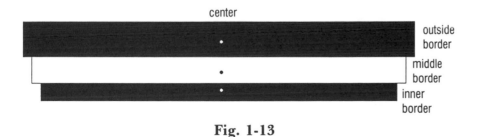

center

outside border

middle border

inner border

Fig. 1-13

of the innermost border. Stop and start sewing ¼″ before the corner edge of the top. The border corners will be flopping loose (Fig. 1-14).

Lay the corner on a padded table or ironing board. Pin the corner in place to keep it from slipping. The seams should be pressed away from the top.

Fig. 1-14

There are several ways to do the next step. I'll describe the method I find easiest. The other methods require special rulers and tools and more careful planning.

Take the border strips that are lying on top and roll them so that the seams line up with those of the strips on the bottom (Fig. 1-15). Place the 45° line from your Quilter's Rule over the corner and check the angle (Fig. 1-16). Press it in place. Pin the borders together. You can sew from the wrong side on the press line by machine or appliqué on the right side by hand.

The third type, a pieced border, is used in some patterns in this book, such as Double Nine-Patch and Lone Star. Specific instructions are given in those chapters.

Fig. 1-15

Fig. 1-16

Basting—You must baste before you can quilt or tie the quilt. It is hard work, best shared with others. Make a super dessert and invite friends over to help. Lay your backing on a tile or hardwood floor right side down. Using wide masking tape, tape the backing to the floor (Fig. 1-17). Stretch it fairly taut. Smooth the batting out on the backing. Lay down top right side up. Smooth from the middle out. Pin, using long quilter's pins, from the center out. The pins should be about 10″ apart.

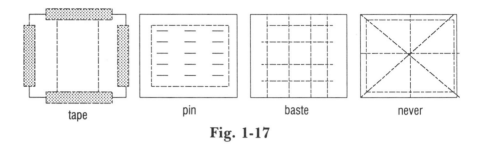

| tape | pin | baste | never |

Fig. 1-17

knot

Fig. 1-18

Take a needle and long basting thread with a knot in the end. I use a tailor's basting stitch that Helen Thompson showed me several years ago (Fig. 1-18). Take a horizontal stitch about ½″ long. Drop down about 2½″ and take another horizontal stitch. The broken line in Fig. 1-18 represents the stitch at the back. Most of your thread is on top of the quilt so that you can avoid stitching in it. Your back will also lie flatter.

Now, using this tailor's basting stitch, stitch from the center to an outside edge. Always work with the grain of the back fabric. Never go from the center to a corner, which will stretch the back fabric on the bias. Make your first four lines, from center to top, to bottom, to right, and to left. Tie a knot as you get to the edge each time. From these four lines stitch in a grid pattern. The spacing should be about 8″. This will allow you to quilt in a hoop or a frame without puckers. I pay my son to baste my quilts. What a job!

Quilting—The fine stitching that connects the back, batt, and top is the quilting. I prefer the old "rocking stitch" method of quilting. It enables me to get a small, even stitch. I use a Q-Snap frame, made from PVC pipe, to hold my work even. Because the frame is square, my fabric is held on the straight of the grain. Books have been written just on quilting. Check your local quilt shop for a copy of *Fine Hand Quilting* by Diana Leone or *How to Improve Your Quilting Stitch* by Ami Simms.

Tying—I call my tying method the Decatur knot because I first saw it in Decatur, Illinois, at the National Quilt Association Show in 1986. It's made with #5 pearl cotton thread and a long, thin needle (5″). Go into the fabric about 3″ away from the *lower right-hand* corner of an intersection (see Fig. 1-19). Keep your needle between the layers of the quilt and make the knot as follows:

1. Come up to the top of the quilt at the intersection.

2. Go down at the *upper left-hand* corner of the intersection. You are now at the back side of the quilt.

3. Come up to the top side of the quilt in the *upper right-hand* corner of the intersection.

4. Take your needle, form a loop between 1 and 2 (see figure), and go through it, forming the knot. Go into the layers again at the *lower left-hand* corner. Slide to the lower right corner of the next intersection. To end, just exit about 3″–4″ from your last knot.

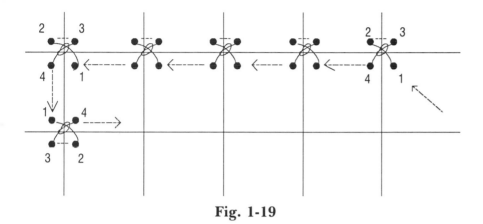

Fig. 1-19

Binding—Cut 2″ strips of fabric, enough to go around the top plus 10″. These should be cut on the straight of grain. Bias strips are necessary only when you are binding curved or scalloped edges. Sew all the strips together to make a long strip. Fold the strip in half along the length, right side out. Sew with ¼″ seam onto the top of quilt, going through all layers. The cut edges are flush with the unfinished edges of the quilt. Start on the bottom, but never at a corner, leaving a 5″ tail of binding. Sew to within ¼″ of the corner, backstitch, and remove from machine. Make a 45° fold and put back in machine to sew the next side. Start sewing ¼″ from the edge and sew side seam, continuing to turn corners as directed. After you have sewn all corners, remove from the machine. Match up the two tails of binding, allowing enough length to complete side. Sew ¼″ seam to connect them. Finish sewing the side. Hand stitch the binding to the back of the quilt. *Warning!* It can take as long to do the hand stitching as it takes to piece the top. I plan on two nights of prime time television to get around the edge. My friend Kerry Dunn has been using this method for years and her bindings are always beautiful.

Supplies for Piecing

Fabric and thread—Choose 45″-wide, 100% cotton fabric. Prewash your fabric in cold water, then run it through the dryer. A quality fabric will save construction time, and the finished quilt will look better and last longer than it would if made with flimsy cottons. Polyester blends are unsuitable for accurate machine piecing because they tend to stretch and pucker when sewn, dull your scissors or rotary cutter, and pill up when washed. Unless you are prepared to shave your quilt after each washing, move on to the cotton shelf. Thread should be a good 100% cotton thread or a cotton-covered polyester. Cheap spun polyesters tend to break as you use them, melt when you iron them, or fall apart when the piece is finished. They also add lint to your machine. Remember you're making an heirloom now!

Rotary cutter and mat—A large or small cutter is fine. Familiarize yourself with the locking device on your cutter, and lock it every time you lay it down. It is amazingly easy to forget. If you are not worried about cutting a finger off, then think about the cutter falling on the floor and ruining the blade. Be careful of cutters that self-lock; in the hands of a child or dropped on the floor, they can be quite dangerous. My preference is the Betty Gall, which has a curved handle for easy cutting while you are sitting and a large blade so you can handle more layers. In my opinion, it has the tightest safety lock on the market, and it is made in the United States. You need a special self-healing mat to use with a rotary cutter. These are widely available in sewing and quilting stores. A large mat is more convenient than a small one. I use one that is 72″ × 36″. In addition I have a 12″ × 12″ mat for squaring up my blocks.

Scissors—Sharp scissors are vital. Mark them so your family will know which scissors not to use. You cannot use the ones you use to cut roses. Small, sharp scissors by the machine are helpful. I am a beginning scissors collector, thanks to Lucy Wheeler, who I think has a pair of every kind of scissors made. It is amazing how the right scissors for a particular project saves time.

Rulers and measuring strips—You will need a thick (at least ⅛″) strip of plastic to cut against. Several possibilities are available:

1. Quilter's Rule—Several sizes, including 12½″ square, 6½″ × 24″, and 4½″ × 14″. The 4½″ × 14″ (Quilter's Rule Junior) is best for squaring a Log Cabin (Fig. 1-20). The ¼″ markings are invaluable, the lines going the length of the ruler are easy on your eyes, and the 45° marks come in very handy. There are grippers on the back so fabric doesn't slip.

2. Log Cabin Strips—These are available in graduated sizes, 1½″, 2″, 2½″, 3″, 3½″, and 4″. For small projects you can use Seminole strips, ½″, ¾″, 1″, and 1¼″.

3. C-Thru or Quilt-N-Sew—2″ × 18″ ruler with a grid of 8 squares to the inch. These are great for checking the accuracy of seams and finished pieces.

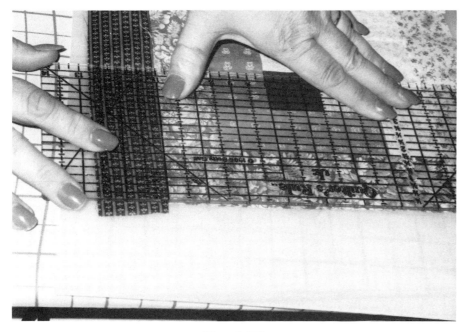

Fig. 1-20

Sewing machine—The most important function of your machine is a wonderful, even straight stitch. Without this you will not be satisfied with your finished product. Accuracy is paramount. The ideal situation is a single-hole needle plate and a straight-stitch presser foot. Check with your sewing machine dealer to see if your brand has these options; on a zigzag machine the wide feed dogs may tend to chew up fabric pieces. A movable needle position is a plus. On a Bernina machine, I piece with the needle in the far right position. This allows me to use the standard zigzag stitch plate. I use a #0 foot and a screw-on seam guide. The needle-stop-down function on the Bernina machine is a big help, as is the knee lift for the presser foot. Most older Singer machines are fine. A Featherweight 221 is a treasure. Clean your machine between quilt tops. A can of compressed air is a great help. Put in a fresh 70(10) or 80(12) needle. If you don't know how to service your machine, have it done yearly.

Seam guide—Some machines have screw-on guides; if not, you can order them from mail-order companies. Don't rely on the etched lines on the needle plate or on masking tape. If you cannot use a screw-on, get a magnetic guide (Dritz). Check the seam frequently. Lorene Gruber says the ABCs of piecing a quilt are: A for Accuracy, B for Be careful to be accurate and C for Continue to be accurate.

For an exact ¼″ seam allowance, first move your needle to the far right (if you can). Lay a ruler on the machine under the needle. For this task, I prefer a Quilt-N-Sew or C-Thru ruler. Slowly lower the needle down to the ¼″ line. Set your seam guide or place a piece of masking tape along the right edge of the ruler. If you use masking tape, place a magnetic seam guide on top of the tape to give your fabric a ridge to move against.

Iron and pad—Pressing will enhance accuracy. Do not use steam while slicing and sewing because it can distort your pieces. I have seen many squares that have become parallelograms with ironing (back-and-forth motion) rather than pressing (up-and-down motion). There are great tabletop ironing boards available. Use a heavy iron so that you will have to press less. With the lightweight irons pressing takes too long.

Long darning needle—Use a needle about 5″ long, sometimes called a doll needle. This will be a guide, a pusher, an extension of your finger and, heaven forbid, your seam ripper! A must! I also use this to tie quilts with the Decatur knot (see Tying on page 12).

Graph paper—Use for all quilts with triangle pieces, including the Little Red School House. Get paper with eight squares to the inch, 17″ × 22″. You can find graph paper at your quilt shop, college bookstore, or office supply store. Make sure the grid is accurate! A cardboard cutting mat scored off in 1″ intervals is not nearly accurate enough.

Miscellaneous—The following items are used only for the Little Red School House. Some may be in your quilt supply box already.

* *Paper punch*—⅛″ is best. Mine is diamond shaped and works perfectly. When I need to see an intersection on a Mylar pattern and mark it on the fabric, I punch a small hole in the plastic and can make a dot with a pencil. A regular punch makes a hole that is too large to mark the intersection accurately.
* *Mylar*—Any clear, template-weight plastic.
* *Art knife*—A fine-tipped blade such as an X-acto or Olfa.
* *Metal-edge ruler*—Mine is cork-backed to prevent slippage. I found it in my husband's tool box.
* *Spray starch*—Helpful to starch the fabric when you cut your roof. I know—I laughed, too, when Paul Pilgrim described how he sprayed until his fabric was as stiff as a board before he marked and cut out his blocks. It does help keep your bias edges from stretching. All of the handling softens up the starch before you are ready to quilt. Give it a try. Spray, then press. I also starch fabric for quick pieced triangles. Be careful of aerosol spray starches, which may damage the fabric. Pump sprays are much better.

Supplies for Finishing

Batting—Make the batt fit the project. Consider the amount of quilting to be done and the time available to quilt. Ninety percent of the pieces I do have Low-Loft by Fairfield in them. It quilts great, drapes nicely, and looks good under dark fabrics.

If I am going to use the Decatur knot and tie my project, I use Fairfield's Extra-Loft. For the special projects that I hand-quilt, I use cotton batting. Fairfield's Cotton Classic is 80% cotton and 20% polyester. It is a little harder to quilt, but the results are worth it. You must quilt close. Warm & Natural cotton, made by Warm Products, Inc., is a needle-punched cotton, with which you do not have to quilt as closely. **Note**: Batting requirements are not included in the yardage charts in this book.

Thread—Use a good quality, 100% cotton quilt thread for quilting. Cotton-covered polyester quilt thread tends to tangle and shred occasionally. Use a #5 pearl cotton thread for tying comforters. Silk finish 100% cotton is great for piecing.

Backing—Don't even think of putting a sheet on the back. It is impossible to quilt and you will need pliers to pull your needle through if you tie the quilt. Get a good quality, 100% cotton fabric. This comes in 45″, 90″, and 108″ widths. Wash, dry, and iron it, and remove selvage edge. If you would like to use a printed fabric (normally 45″ wide) on the back, you will have to piece the back together. The average cost is about ten dollars more. If you don't want your quilting to show on the back, that would be the best way to go. I wait until the top is finished before I get the back, unless I know that I want one of the fabrics from the top—better get it before it's gone.

Backing fabric is not included in the fabric requirements charts in this book. You can use one of the fabrics you are using in the quilt for your backing. Quilt backs are also available in 90″ and 108″ widths. Always measure the finished quilt top, then add at least 4″ to the length and width. Unless you are using 90″ or 108″ wide fabric, you will need to sew together two or three widths, depending on the size of your quilt. Here are some very general guidelines for the amount of backing to buy:

Crib	1½–1¾ yards 44″ wide
Twin	5¾ yards 44″ wide or 2¾ yards 90″ wide
Full	6¼ yards 44″ wide or 3¼ yards 90″ or 108″ wide
Queen/King	9½ yards 44″ wide or 3¼ yards 108″ wide

Needles—The number on quilting needles gets higher as the needles get smaller. For a beginner I recommend a 9 between. A between is a quilting needle. As the saying goes, "The shorter the needle, the shorter the stitch." Try to use a 10 or a 12. A quilter doesn't need room on the needle for his or her thumb! The long darning needle (see page 16) is used for tying as well as guiding the fabric through the sewing machine. A 5″ length is best. Start your quilt with a new needle on your machine. I use a 70(10)H or 80(12)H Bernina or Schmetz. They also work on Singer Featherweights and hold their point longer than other brands.

BEGINNERS'
QUILTS BY THE SLICE

Chapter 2

Rail Fence

Rail Fence quilts (Fig. 2-1) date back to the mid-1860s. They were and are confused with Log Cabins, in part because of the coloring similarities in the Rail Fence and the Log Cabin Straight Furrow design. Both use a small rail or log that makes up the block. The Rail Fence was a good way for pioneer women to use up their scraps of fabric, which were divided into piles of light, medium, and dark. For Quilts by the Slice you use longer pieces of fabric to speed up piecing.

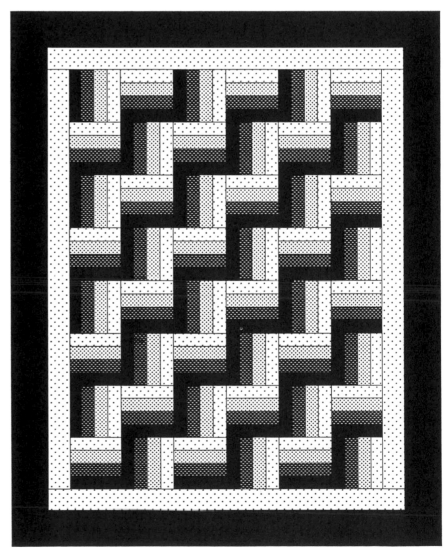

Fig. 2-1

This is an easy project for teaching children how to piece. They do all the sewing and I do the slicing. When one of my daughters was seven, she made a Rail Fence doll quilt using a 6″ block.

The quilt in this chapter uses four fabrics: a dark, two mediums, and a light. But a Rail Fence can also be made using three fabrics: try a light, medium, and dark. Cut them all 2½″ wide. Follow directions below for assembly, then slice your three-color blocks 6½″ square. If you decide to try the three-color 6″ block, follow these guidelines to make the size you want:

Rail Fence, Three Colors, 6″ Blocks

	Twin	Full	Queen	King
Blocks across	9	10	13	16
Blocks down	14	14	15	16
Total blocks	126	140	195	256
Fabric	3 yds each	3½ yds each	4 yds each	4½ yds each

Slicing

The dark and light slices are twice as long as your mediums. Slice your border and set it aside. Cut dark and light fabric strips in half lengthwise. This will make them the same length as the mediums. All should be the same length for piecing.

Dimensions of Quilts, Rail Fence

	Crib	Twin	Full	Queen	King
Finished size	43″ × 55″	68″ × 100″	76″ × 100″	92″ × 108″	110″ × 110″
Size of blocks	6″	8″	8″	8″	8″
Total number of blocks	48	77	88	120	144
Number of blocks across	6	7	8	10	12
Number of blocks down	8	11	11	12	12
Borders (finished size)	1½″, 2″	2½″, 3½″	2″, 4″	2″, 4″	2½″, 4½″

Fabric Requirements, Rail Fence

	Crib	Twin	Full	Queen	King
Dark	1½ yds	3 yds	3½ yds	4½ yds	4½ yds
Medium 1	¾ yd	1½ yds	1¾ yds	2¼ yds	2¼ yds
Medium 2	¾ yd	1½ yds	1¾ yds	2¼ yds	2¼ yds
Light	1½ yds	3 yds	3½ yds	4½ yds	4½ yds

Slicing Information for Blocks, Rail Fence

	Crib	Twin	Full	Queen	King
Dark					
Number of slices	6	7	7	8	8
Size of slices	2″ × 54″	2½″ × 108″	2½″ × 126″	2½″ × 162″	2½″ × 162″
Medium 1					
Number of slices	12	13	13	15	16
Size of slices	2″ × 27″	2½″ × 54″	2½″ × 63″	2½″ × 81″	2½″ × 81″
Medium 2					
Number of slices	12	13	13	15	16
Size of slices	2″ × 27″	2½″ × 54″	2½″ × 63″	2½″ × 81″	2½″ × 81″
Light					
Number of slices	6	7	7	8	8
Size of slices	2″ × 54″	2½″ × 108″	2½″ × 126″	2½″ × 162″	2½″ × 162″

Slicing Information for Borders and Binding, Rail Fence

	Crib	Twin	Full	Queen	King
Dark (border 2)					
Number of border strips	4	4	4	4	4
Size of slices	2″ × 54″	4″ × 108″	4½″ × 108″	4½″ × 108″	5″ × 112″
Dark (binding)					
Number of binding strips	4	4	3*	8	9
Size of slices	2″ × 54″	2″ × 108″	2″ × 126″	2″ × 54″	2″ × 50″
Light (border 1)					
Number of border strips	4	4	4	4	4
Size of slices	2″ × 54″	3″ × 108″	2½″ × 108″	2½″ × 108″	3″ × 108″

* There will be a 2½″ × 63″ slice left over from piecing. Trim it to 2″ and add to binding.

Piecing

1. Using a ¼″ seam, sew a dark strip to a medium 1 strip (Fig. 2-2) the following number of times:

Crib	Twin	Full	Queen	King
12	13	13	15	16

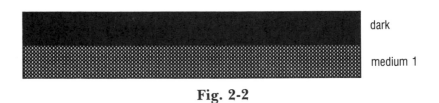

Fig. 2-2

Press seams toward dark.

2. Sew a medium 2 strip to a light strip (Fig. 2-3) the same number of times as in the preceding step.

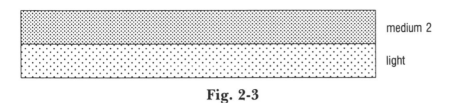

medium 2

light

Fig. 2-3

Press seams toward medium 2.

3. Sew medium 1 to medium 2 for all the units you just made (see Fig. 2-4). Press this seam toward medium 1.

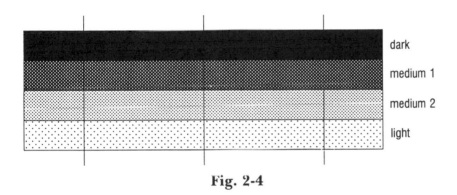

dark

medium 1

medium 2

light

Fig. 2-4

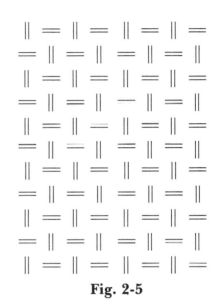

Fig. 2-5

4. Measure the widths of your units. They should be 8½″ wide (6½″ for crib). You will now cut across the strips to make blocks the same width as the strip unit. Check the width of your strip units carefully. If they come up short—say, 8¼″—you must cut your slices 8¼″, not 8½″.

5. Using a square ruler, slice the units into squares based on the width of the strips (Fig. 2-4) until you have the following number of blocks:

Fig. 2-6

	Crib	Twin	Full	Queen	King
	48	77	88	120	144

6. You are now ready to make pairs. At this point take the time to draw out your quilt. Use two double lines as a symbol for each block. The odd rows always start with a vertical block, the even with a horizontal. For example, a full-size quilt drawing is shown in Fig. 2-5. Now circle all pairs that look like Fig. 2-6. Fig. 2-7 shows the full-size quilt drawing with pairs circled. Always key in on the darkest rectangles in the blocks. Lay one block (dark at the

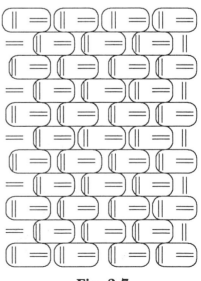

Fig. 2-7

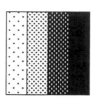

Fig. 2-8

Fig. 2-9

right) right side up on the machine (Fig. 2-8). Lay the second block with dark on the bottom, wrong side up on top of the first block. Sew a ¼″ seam (Fig. 2-9). Make the following number of pairs:

	Crib	Twin	Full	Queen	King
	20	33	39	54	66

You will have the following number of blocks left after your pairs are made:

	Crib	Twin	Full	Queen	King
	8	11	10	12	12

7. If you examine your drawing again, you will see that you need the following number of groups of four (two pairs) (Fig. 2-10).

	Crib	Twin	Full	Queen	King
	8	11	17	24	30

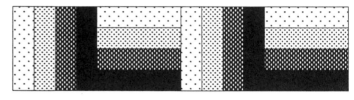

Fig. 2-10

You will have some pairs left over as well as some single blocks.

8. Next, sew your rows. Working left to right, the odd rows, starting with row 1, will begin with a vertical block with the dark on the right. The even rows, starting with row 2, begin with a horizontal block with the dark on the bottom (Fig. 2-11). The extra pairs and extra single blocks will help you fill out the rows. Sew on the extras at the beginning and ends of the rows according to your drawing (Fig. 2-7).

Row 1

Row 2

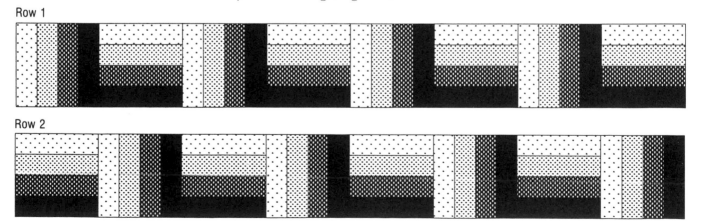

Fig. 2-11

9. Sew your rows together, locking the seams together at each block intersection. If your machine can stop with the needle in the down position, all the better at this point. Leave your needle down in the fabric while you check the next intersection. It is possible to ease ¼″ to ½″ if you have 8″ to do it in. You cannot ease anything if you wait until you get to the intersection.

Each row should now have the following number of blocks across:

	Crib	Twin	Full	Queen	King
	6	7	8	10	12

and the following number of blocks down:

	Crib	Twin	Full	Queen	King
	8	11	11	12	12

This is a good time to press your rows. Looking at the back of the row you will see that the seams of the horizontal blocks want to go toward the vertical blocks—let them! This will make your seams lock together as you sew your rows together.

10. Before you get ready to put on your borders, measure the length and width of your quilt through the center of the top. That will determine the length of your first side border. First sew a light border strip, sewing the long sides first. Press the seams toward the border. Square up the top and bottom of that border. Sew on the top and bottom piece. After you have pressed and squared those pieces, repeat the process for the dark (see Chapter 1, page 9, for more information about borders).

Finishing

Now you are ready to baste. Or talk someone else into doing it! Review Chapter 1 for your quilting or tying options. After you have quilted or tied, put on the binding as described in Chapter 1.

Chapter 3

Log Cabin

Log Cabin with 2½" Strips

The Log Cabin dates back to the early 1800s. It was a favorite of pioneer women, because by using this pattern they could make good use of light and dark scraps of fabric (Fig. 3-1). Most quilts dating to the middle or late 1800s have either red or yellow centers. It is said that the red center represented the hearth of the home. The yellow was frequently used when the man was away from the house. Possibly he was working another farm or on the railroad, or was off to war. The yellow represented the lantern left waiting in the window. In any case, the logs (small strips of fabric) were divided into piles of lights and darks and then sewn around the center.

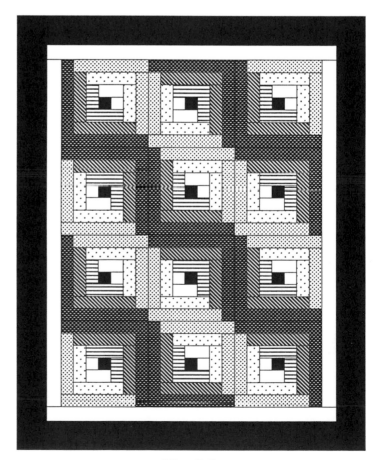

Fig. 3-1

Today we still choose lights and darks for a Log Cabin. A good rule is to have your darkest light be lighter than your lightest dark. Try to avoid stripes. Choose a pleasing color range, with the colors flowing from one fabric to the next. Try using large floral prints and colors with a dramatic difference for a beautiful contemporary design. I frequently use all one fabric for the light side of the quilt to assure a difference between my light and dark sides.

My second Log Cabin (see the Introduction about my first) was a red, white, and blue queen-size top made with 1½" slices. I made two mistakes with it. One was to tell my husband that he could have it. (He has to see some benefit from all this fabric.) The second mistake came when, in a weak moment, I sold it. In the meantime I made a cover for a friend's deacon's bench out of the same fabric, ¾" slices, 70 blocks. Never again. I also made one with 2" slices, same fabric. Neither size satisfied my husband. He wanted an exact repeat of the original, so back to the 1½" slices. I donated the pieced top with 2" slices to the local elementary school raffle and completed Jim's quilt top. It sat for three years before I started to quilt it. But it's finally finished and on the bed.

By now, I have made more than 100 Log Cabins and seen about 5,000 made in class. It is still one of my favorite quilts. The blue and muslin Log Cabin shown in the color section is the one I am most proud of. I made it this year for my friends Bill and Lucy Wheeler of Lexington, Kentucky. It is a reproduction of an antique quilt and measures 112" × 126". There are 288 blocks with 1" strips. I used a blue star fabric made by Marcus Brothers, three red solid fabrics, and muslin from five different bolts. It is so beautiful.

In figuring yardage for the 2½" Log Cabin, I chose light 1, dark 1, and dark 3 for the borders. They work most of the time for me. If that doesn't suit your project, feel free to change them.

I frequently use the center fabric for the first border. You can subtract ¾ yard from the first light or the first dark fabric if you decide not to use it for a border.

Yardage and slicing directions for the 2½" Log Cabin are given in the charts. At the end of this section I have also included information for a 2" strip. It takes longer to make, but it gives you greater design potential.

Before you begin, consider the layout of the quilt. There are several possibilities (see pages 32–34). If you decide on a Barn Raising design, you will need an even number of blocks in an even number of rows. The queen-size quilt normally calls for 30 blocks (5 × 6). For a Barn Raising pattern, though, you will need to make six extra blocks for 36 blocks. Increase your yardage figures by ¼ yard each for piecing. You may also need to reduce the width of your borders.

Slicing

All of the fabrics here are cut on the lengthwise grain except the center, which I cut on the crosswise grain if I use only ¼ yd. I frequently change this, as I mentioned earlier, and put it in the border, in which case I use a border length and cut it on the length. Each fabric except the center will be used twice.

Dimensions of Quilts, Log Cabin, 2½″ Strips

	Twin	Full	Queen	King
Finished size	64″ × 92″	77″ × 105″	94″ × 108″	110″ × 110″
Size of blocks	14″	14″	14″	14″
Total number of blocks	15	24	30	36
Number of blocks across	3	4	5	6
Number of blocks down	5	6	6	6
Borders (finished size)	3″, 3½″, 4½″	3″, 3½″, 4″	3″, 4″, 5″	3″, 4″, 6″

Fabric Requirements, Log Cabin, 2½″ Strips

	Twin	Full	Queen	King
Center	¼ yd	¼ yd	¼ yd	¼ yd
Light 1 (lightest)	1½ yds	1½ yds	1¾ yds	1¾ yds
Light 2	1 yd	1¼ yds	1¼ yds	1¼ yds
Light 3	1¼ yds	1¼ yds	1½ yds	1¾ yds
Dark 1	1½ yds	3 yds	3 yds	3 yds
Dark 2	1 yd	1¼ yds	1¼ yds	1¾ yds
Dark 3 (darkest)	3½ yds	4 yds	4½ yds	5 yds

Slicing Information for Blocks, Log Cabin, 2½″ Strips

Note: Before slicing, tear the Dark 3 for the queen size into two pieces: 45″ and 108″. For the king size, tear the Dark 3 into two pieces: 110″ and 65″.

	Twin	Full	Queen	King
Center				
Number of slices	1	2	2	3
Size of slices	2½″ × 42″	2½″ × 42″	2½″ × 42″	2½″ × 42″
Light 1				
Number of slices	3	4	4	5
Size of slices	2½″ × 54″	2½″ × 54″	2½″ × 63″	2½″ × 63″
Light 2				
Number of slices	8	9	13	15
Size of slices	2½″ × 36″	2½″ × 45″	2½″ × 45″	2½″ × 45″
Light 3				
Number of slices	10	14	14	14
Size of slices	2½″ × 45″	2½″ × 45″	2½″ × 54″	2½″ × 63″

	Twin	Full	Queen	King
Dark 1				
Number of slices	4	3	3	4
Size of slices	2½″ × 54″	2½″ × 108″	2½″ × 108″	2½″ × 108″
Dark 2				
Number of slices	10	11	14	13
Size of slices	2½″ × 36″	2½″ × 45″	2½″ × 45″	2½″ × 63″
Dark 3				
Number of slices	5	6	15	6
Size of slices	2½″ × 108″	2½″ × 126″	2½″ × 45″	2½″ × 110″
Number of slices	—	—	3	9
Size of slices	—	—	2½″ × 108″	2½″ × 65″

Slicing Information for Borders and Binding, Log Cabin, 2½″ Strips

See note in preceding chart about tearing fabrics before slicing.

	Twin	Full	Queen	King
Light 1 (border 1)				
Number of slices	8*	8*	8*	8*
Size of slices	3½″ × 54″	3½″ × 54″	3½″ × 63″	3½″ × 63″
Dark 1 (border 2)				
Number of slices	8*	4	4	4
Size of slices	4″ × 54″	4″ × 108″	4½″ × 108″	4½″ × 108″
Dark 3 (border 3)				
Number of slices	4	4	4	4
Size of slices	5″ × 108″	4½″ × 108″	5½″ × 108″	6½″ × 110″
Dark 3 (binding)				
Number of slices	4	4	4	7*
Size of slices	2″ × 108″	2″ × 108″	2″ × 108″	2″ × 65″

*These borders will be seamed unless you are using a border length.

Piecing

1. Sew the center strip to the light 1 slice, right sides together, using ¼″ seam. Cut off any excess light 1. Follow the chart below for number of times to sew two strips together:

Twin	Full	Queen	King
1	2	2	3

2. Go to the iron. Place strip center color down. Lift up the first light strip and use the tip of the iron to press the seam (you are pressing on the right side of the fabric). Press the seam away from the center color.

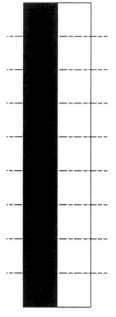

Fig. 3-2

Fig. 3-3

3. Lay the ironed strip on the cutting mat. With your rotary cutter and the Quilter's Rule Jr., slice across the strips every 2½″ (Fig. 3-2). You need the following number of slices (pieces):

	Twin	Full	Queen	King
	15	24	30	36

Make one extra slice. It is easier to throw away a bad block than to rip it apart.

4. Take another light 1 strip and lay it on the machine, right side up. (Sewing the wrong side together is a frequent mistake.) This is the second time this fabric is to be used. Lay your pieced center slices on top, right side down, light side at top. You must see the seam on top, pointing up toward the light side, as shown in Fig. 3-3. (Hold that seam down with your 5″ needle—you don't want the presser foot to flip that seam.) Fill up your strips with blocks, leaving a scant ¼″ space between blocks. If a block does not totally fit on a strip, begin a new strip. Sew with a ¼″ seam, spacing as before.

5. Cut between the blocks with sharp scissors. I lay it across my lap, strip down, block on top, seam toward me. Or you can fold the strip, line up the blocks, and cut.

6. Go to the iron. Lay the center two squares down with the longer strip on top. Lift up the strip and press away from the seam. Press seams away from the center.

7. Now it is time to square your block. I do it each time after I press the new addition to the block. Lay your block on the small trimming board with the new piece closest to you. You will square the right-hand side of the block. Place your Jr. Rule on top of the block. (The Jr. Rule has the best ¼″ markings, but you can use any clear straightedge.) Seam A (Fig. 3-4) should align with a black vertical line on the ruler. Have a horizontal line on Seam B at the 2¼″ position. With your rotary cutter trim the right-hand side. Squaring up your blocks will add about one hour to your quilt, but it's worth the time and money you have in it. It will make it so much easier to sew your blocks together later.

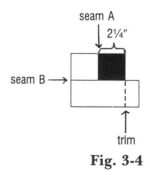

Fig. 3-4

8. Lay a strip of dark 1 on the machine, right side up. Put the pieced blocks on top of the strip, with the last sewn piece at the top (Fig. 3-5). The seam (not shown in Fig. 3-5) will be pointing up. This is the side you just squared. Sew with a ¼″ seam, spacing blocks ¼″ apart. Cut the blocks apart as before.

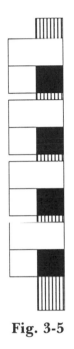

Fig. 3-5

9. Press these units with the block underneath and the strip on top. Press the seam away from the center. Square again. The last strip you sewed on is closest to you. You are still squaring to 2¼″. Always look at your block from the back (wrong side) to determine which side you are sewing on. From this point on, you will always sew on the side with two seams on the outside edge, one up and one down. Looking at the back of your block, you can see that you are working in a counterclockwise direction.

10. Place a strip of dark 1 on the machine right side up. This is the second time that this fabric is to be used. Lay the pieced blocks on top with the last piece that was sewn (dark 1) on top (Fig. 3-6). There should be two seams on the right, one up and one down (not shown in fig.). Sew all blocks onto strips of the first dark. Cut them apart.

11. Go to the iron and press as before. The pressing gets easier as your block gets bigger. After ironing, square your blocks (Fig. 3-7). As you move ahead, be sure to take the following into consideration:

✱ Each time you press your block, check to see if the block is square. If not, trim and correct problem.

✱ Be careful cutting blocks apart.

✱ Don't stretch as you press.

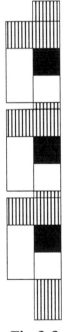

Fig 3-6

Fig. 3-7

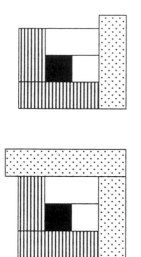

12. The next fabric used is light 2. Use it twice (Fig. 3-8). Then you will use the dark 2 (Fig. 3-9), light 3 (Fig. 3-10), and dark 3 (Fig. 3-11). Each color will be used twice. Your blocks are now finished.

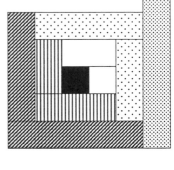

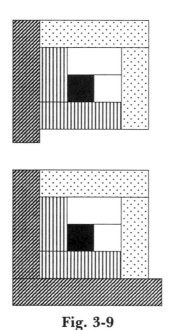

Fig. 3-8

Fig. 3-9   **Fig. 3-10**

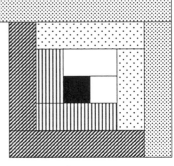

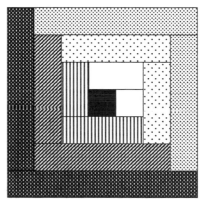

Fig. 3-11

13. Give each block a final pressing. With a straightedge and rotary cutter, make sure your blocks are square.

14. Lay your blocks on the floor and choose your design. There are many ways to set together a Log Cabin. The three most common are:

✳ *Continental*—In the Continental design, each block is laid down identically (Fig. 3-12). For example, the light corner of the

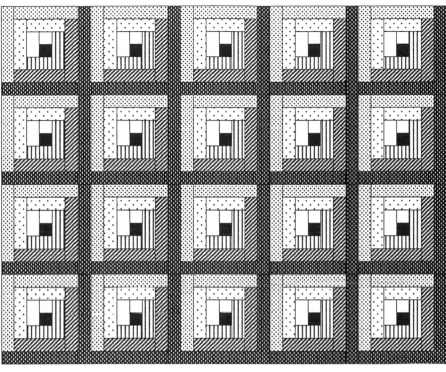

Fig. 3-12

block is always in the upper left position. The blocks in the Continental design look as if they have sashing around them. I usually add a first border of my third dark on the two sides that have the light 3 on the outside. The blue baby quilt shown in the color pages has extra borders to balance it out.

* *Straight Furrows*—The Straight Furrows design is made when the blocks are turned 180 degrees (Fig. 3-13). For example, the light corner of the first block is in the upper left position and in the next block it is in the lower right.

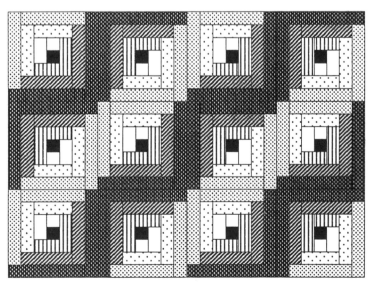

Fig. 3-13

❋ *Barn Raising*—The Barn Raising design is laid out with light and dark diamonds (Fig. 3-14). For example, all four dark corners touch in the center and appear surrounded by a light diamond. Remember, you must have an even number of blocks per row and an even number of rows. I used this for the scrap black and khaki piece in the color pages.

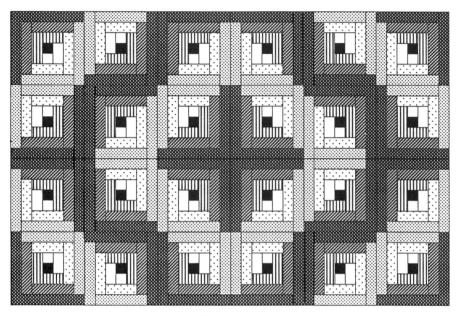

Fig. 3-14

15. Sew together the blocks that make up a row. As you do this, pay attention to the seams. Sew them in the direction that they have been pressed. As you start to sew two blocks together, check to see if you need to do any easing. When you are at the last inch of a seam, it's too late to ease.

16. After you have sewn the blocks together into rows, sew the rows together. As you do this, the seam between the two blocks should be going in the opposite direction of the one under it, one up and one down.

17. Now it is time to make borders. I never miter the borders of a Log Cabin. I use what I call Log Cabin corners. The strips for the first border (light 1) may need to be sewn together to make them long enough, if you have not used a border length. The seam will not be seen on many floral patterns. Measure the length of the quilt through the middle. Cut your first two border pieces this long. They should measure approximately:

	Twin	Full	Queen	King
	70½″	84½″	84½″	84½″

18. Sew on the side border pieces with ¼″ seams. Press the seams toward the borders.

19. Square the corners by laying your ruler on top and trimming off the excess. Now measure the width of the quilt through the middle, including the borders you have just sewn on. Cut the remaining first border pieces this length.

20. Sew on the top and bottom borders and press toward the border. Trim the corners before you sew on your next borders.

21. Sew the second border (dark 1) on long sides first, then top and bottom. Press and square after each turn.

22. Sew on last border (dark 3), sides first and then top and bottom.

Finishing

You are now ready to quilt or tie your top. I like to quilt a Log Cabin in a spiral design from the center out. I use ¼" masking tape to mark the design. I quilt the borders as though they were a solid piece of fabric. For this I use 1" or 2" masking tape.

If you prefer to tie your quilt, review Chapter 1.

Log Cabin with 2" Strips

This Log Cabin will take you longer to make than the 2½" strip. Your block is smaller, so you need more blocks. There is a payoff in the increased design possibilities. The yardage is similar; however, more seams do take more fabric.

I've also included information for a crib-size Log Cabin here. I do not think it looks quite right with the larger, 2½" strips. This is the quilt I make most frequently for gifts. I also make it to try out color. I have made about fifty crib-size Log Cabins. Have fun!

I like to use the center fabric as the inner border and binding on the crib sizes. I make so many Log Cabins that I always have solids in border lengths, so I cut it on the length. I would suggest, however, that for the crib size you cut carefully on the width so that you can get by on ¾ yard. Everything except the third dark will be sliced on the width for the crib size. You must straighten the grain first if your fabric store cuts the fabric instead of tearing it. I have allowed a little extra for that reason.

The full size 2"-strip Log Cabin has 30 blocks, but if you want to make a Barn Raising pattern, you will need to make 36 blocks (see page 27 and 34). Unless you're making a crib-size Log Cabin, slice all of your borders first, on the length.

Construct this Log Cabin the same as with the 2½" strips. You might even want to try 1½" strips; same method, more blocks. The following charts give all the information you'll need.

Dimensions of Quilts, Log Cabin, 2″ Strips

	Crib	Twin	Full	Queen	King
Finished size	41½″ × 52″	67″ × 88″	77½″ × 88″	86″ × 107″	110″ × 110″
Size of blocks	10½″	10½″	10½″	10½″	10½″
Total number of blocks	12	24	30	48	64
Number of blocks across	3	4	5	6	8
Number of blocks down	4	6	6	8	8
Borders (finished size)	2″, 3″	3″, 4″, 5½″	3″, 4″, 5½″	3″, 4″, 4½″	3″, 4½″, 5½″

Fabric Requirements, Log Cabin, 2″ Strips

	Crib	Twin	Full	Queen	King
Center	¾ yd	¼ yd	¼ yd	¼ yd	¼ yd
Light 1 (lightest)	¼ yd	1½ yds	1½ yds	1½ yds	2 yds
Light 2	⅓ yd	1 yd	1 yd	1 yd	1½ yds
Light 3	½ yd	1¼ yds	1½ yds	1½ yds	2 yds
Dark 1	⅓ yd	1½ yds	2 yds	3 yds	3 yds
Dark 2	⅓ yd	1 yd	1¼ yds	1½ yds	1½ yds
Dark 3 (darkest)	1½ yds	3½ yds	3½ yds	4½ yds	4¾ yds

Slicing Information for Blocks, Log Cabin, 2″ Strips

Note: Before slicing, you will need to tear some fabric as follows: For the queen size, tear Dark 3 into two pieces: 108″ and 54″. Use the 54″ slices first. For the king size, tear Dark 3 into two pieces: 112″ and 59″. Use 59″ slices first.

	Crib	Twin	Full	Queen	King
Center					
Number of slices	1	2	2	3	4
Size of slices	2″ × 42″	2″ × 42″	2″ × 42″	2″ × 42″	2″ × 42″
Light 1					
Number of slices	3	4	5	6	6
Size of slices	2″ × 42″	2″ × 54″	2″ × 54″	2″ × 54″	2″ × 72″
Light 2					
Number of slices	5	9	12	17	16
Size of slices	2″ × 42″	2″ × 36″	2″ × 36″	2″ × 36″	2″ × 54″
Light 3					
Number of slices	7	12	14	19	18
Size of slices	2″ × 42″	2″ × 45″	2″ × 54″	2″ × 54″	2″ × 72″

	Crib	Twin	Full	Queen	King
Dark 1					
Number of slices	5	5	4	5	6
Size of slices	2″ × 42″	2″ × 54″	2″ × 72″	2″ × 108″	2″ × 108″
Dark 2					
Number of slices	5	13	14	16	19
Size of slices	2″ × 42″	2″ × 36″	2″ × 45″	2″ × 54″	2″ × 54″
Dark 3					
Number of slices	7	5	6	2	3
Size of slices	2″ × 54″	2″ × 126″	2″ × 126″	2″ × 108″	2″ × 112″
Number of slices	—	—	—	21	21
Size of slices	—	—	—	2″ × 54″	2″ × 59″

Slicing Information for Borders and Binding, Log Cabin, 2″ Strips

See note in preceding chart about tearing fabrics before slicing.

	Crib	Twin	Full	Queen	King
Center	(border 1)				
Number of slices	4*	—	—	—	—
Size of slices	2½″ × 42″	—	—	—	—
Center	(binding)				
Number of slices	4	—	—	—	—
Size of slices	2″ × 42″	—	—	—	—
Light 1		(border 1)	(border 1)	(border 1)	(border 1)
Number of slices	—	8*	8*	8*	6
Size of slices	—	3½″ × 54″	3½″ × 54″	3½″ × 54″	3½″ × 72″
Dark 1		(border 2)	(border 2)	(border 2)	(border 2)
Number of slices	—	7*	6	4	4
Size of slices	—	4½″ × 54″	4½″ × 72″	4½″ × 108″	5″ × 108″
Dark 3	(border 2)	(border 3)	(border 3)	(border 3)	(border 3)
Number of slices	4*	4	4*	4	4
Size of slices	3½″ × 54″	6″ × 108″	6″ × 108″	5″ × 108″	6″ × 115″
Dark 3		(binding)	(binding)	(binding)	(binding)
Number of slices	—	2	3	4	4
Size of slices	—	2″ × 126″	2″ × 126″	2″ × 108″	2″ × 112″

*These borders will be seamed unless you are using a border length.

Chapter 4

Single Irish Chain

The Irish Chain is one of America's oldest pieced quilts (Fig. 4-1). It is a simple pattern made by setting Nine-Patch blocks with plain blocks. One reason for its popularity is the flexibility of the design.

Fig. 4-1

I first saw this pattern in an old *Quilter's Newsletter* article by Barbara Johannah. The advent of the rotary cutter made this quilt a quick project. It makes a super quick baby quilt if tied with the Decatur knot (see pages 12–13).

Because the Irish Chain is set with an alternate block, you must use an odd number of rows and an odd number of blocks in a row. For example, if you start a row with a patched block, you cannot end it with solid block. The quilt will look off-balance.

The grain of the fabric is particularly important for this quilt. The lengthwise grain of the fabric should run the length of the bed.

Slicing

Slice fabric according to the following charts. Set aside the slices for solid blocks.

Dimensions of Quilts, Single Irish Chain

	Crib	Twin	Full	Queen/King
Finished size	40″ × 52″	58″ × 94″	77″ × 95″	97″ × 115″
Size of blocks	6″	9″	9″	9″
Total number of blocks	35	45	63	99
Number of blocks across	5	5	7	9
Number of blocks down	7	9	9	11
Number of pieced blocks	18	23	32	50
Number of solid blocks	17	22	31	49
Borders (finished size)	2″, 3″	3″, 3½″	3″, 4″	1″, 3″, 4″

Fabric Requirements, Single Irish Chain

	Crib	Twin	Full	Queen/King
Nine-Patch dark chain	1½ yds	3 yds	3½ yds	5 yds
Nine-Patch light and background	1¾ yds	4 yds	5 yds	7 yds

Slicing Information for Blocks, Single Irish Chain

Note: Before slicing you will need to tear some fabric as follows: For the twin size, tear light fabric into two pieces: 108″ and 36″. For the full size, tear light fabric into two pieces: 126″ and 54″. For the queen/king size, tear light fabric into three pieces: 117″, 63″, and 72″. Also for the queen/king, tear dark fabric into two pieces: 117″ and 63″.

	Crib	Twin	Full	Queen/King
Dark				
Number of slices	5	5	5	5
Size of slices	2½″ × 54″	3½″ × 96″	3½″ × 126″	3½″ × 117″
Number of slices	—	—	—	5
Size of slices	—	—	—	3½″ × 63″
Light for Nine-Patch				
Number of slices	4	4	4	4
Size of slices	2½″ × 54″	3½″ × 96″	3½″ × 126″	3½″ × 117″
Number of slices	—	—	—	4
Size of slices	—	—	—	3½″ × 63″
Light for solid blocks				
Number of slices	2	1	1	2
Size of slices	6½″ × 63″	9½″ × 108″	9½″ × 126″	9½″ × 63″
Number of slices	—	4	4	4
Size of slices	—	9½″ × 36″	9½″ × 54″	9½″ × 72″
Number of slices				1
Size of slices				9½″ × 117″

Slicing Information for Borders and Binding, Single Irish Chain

See note in preceding chart about tearing fabrics before slicing.

	Crib	Twin	Full	Queen/King
Dark (border 1)				
Number of slices	4	4	4	4
Size of slices	2½″ × 54″	3½″ × 108″	3½″ × 108″	1½″ × 117″
Number of slices	—	—	—	4*
Size of slices	—	—	—	4½″ × 117″
Light (border 2)				
Number of slices	4	4	4	4
Size of slices	3½″ × 54″	4″ × 108″	4½″ × 108″	3½″ × 117″
Dark (binding)				
Number of slices	4	3	4	7
Size of slices	2″ × 54″	2″ × 108″	2″ × 108″	2″ × 63″

* Use 1½″ dark as first border and 4½″ dark as third border.

Fig. 4-2

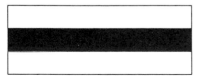

Fig. 4-3

Piecing

1. Sew one strip of light fabric between two strips of dark fabric to form Unit 1 (Fig. 4-2). Make two of these units. (For queen/king size, make two long units and two short units). Press seams toward the dark fabric. Make sure you don't fold excess fabric into the seam.

2. To make Unit 2 sew one strip of dark fabric between two strips of light fabric (Fig. 4-3). Make one of these units. (For the queen/king size, make one long unit and one short.) Again, press toward the dark fabric.

3. Slice across the pressed units using your rotary cutter (Fig. 4-4). The width of each slice should be:

Crib	Twin	Full	Queen/King
2½″	3½″	3½″	3½″

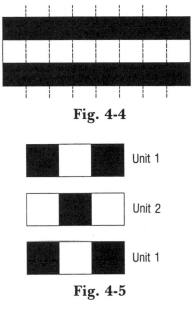

Fig. 4-4

4. The Irish Chain pieced blocks are made up of three slices (Fig. 4-5):

two slices Unit 1 + one slice Unit 2

You will need the following number of Unit 1 slices:

Crib	Twin	Full	Queen/King
36	46	64	100

You will need the following number of Unit 2 slices:

Crib	Twin	Full	Queen/King
18	23	32	50

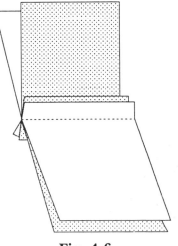

Fig. 4-5

To sew the block together, you must have your Unit 1 slice on top and the Unit 2 slice on the bottom, right sides together. Take your fingers and feel the ridge where the seams lock together (Fig. 4-6). It must feel smooth. The top seam of Unit 1 will be pointed toward the sewing machine.

5. After sewing through the first seam, adjust the next seam so it lies flat, then finish sewing to the end of the slice.

6. Continue to sew sliced pairs without clipping threads between units, you have used all slices of Unit 2. This is called chain piecing. It is faster, saves thread, and keeps your needle from coming unthreaded. Clip the threads to separate the pairs before you press them.

Fig. 4-6

7. Press seam toward Unit 1 slice. Lay one of the sewn pairs on the ironing pad with Unit 1 on top. Slide the tip of the iron between the two units, pushing Unit 1 over. That will make the seam lie toward Unit 1.

8. Sew on the remaining Unit 1 slice, right sides together, with the Unit 1 slice on top. Press as above. From the back the seams look like Fig. 4-7.

9. Now take the fabric that will make up your solid block. The width of this is 9½″ (crib size, 6½″). Lay a slice on your sewing machine right side up. Put a pieced block on top, right side down.

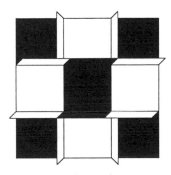

Fig. 4-7

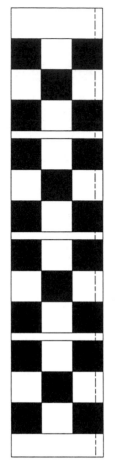

Fig. 4-8

Fig. 4-9

Units 1 and 2 should be lying horizontally. Leave a slight space between blocks (Fig. 4-8). Sew the following number of blocks:

	Crib	Twin	Full	Queen/King
	14	18	27	44

With sharp scissors, cut between the blocks. Now you have pairs of pieced blocks and solid blocks (Fig. 4-9). Press seam toward solid block.

10. Square the block using your rotary cutter. You should have extra pieced blocks as follows:

	Crib	Twin	Full	Queen/King
	4	5	5	6

11. Take the remaining 9½″ strip of fabric and cut it into 9½″ squares, to make the following number of solid blocks.

	Crib	Twin	Full	Queen/King
	3	4	4	5

12. Sew your pairs together to make:

	Crib	Twin	Full	Queen/King
	7 rows of 4 blocks	9 rows of 4 blocks	9 rows of 6 blocks	11 rows of 8 blocks

Each odd-numbered row must begin and end with a pieced block (Fig. 4-10). Therefore, sew the extra pieced blocks on the end of these rows. Each even-numbered row must begin and end with a solid block (Fig. 4-11). Therefore, sew a solid block to the beginning of each even row. Press all seams toward solid blocks.

Row 1 (odd)

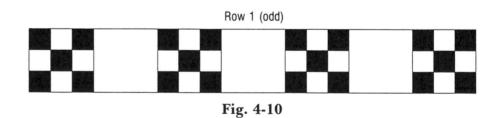

Fig. 4-10

Row 2 (even)

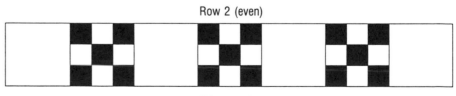

Fig. 4-11

13. Sew your rows together. Lock your seams in the same way as when you sewed your slices together (Fig. 4-6).

14. To make the borders, measure the center length of your top. Cut two of your dark border strips to that length. Sew them on the two long sides of the pieced quilt top. Press seams toward border. Square off the top and bottom edges of that border. Now measure the center width of quilt (including border). Cut remaining dark border strips to that length and sew on the top and bottom. Sew on light border in the same way.

Finishing

If you are making the queen/king quilt you will use a narrow dark border first, then the light and finally your large dark. Your top is ready to be basted. Review basting, tying, and quilting options in Chapter 1.

Chapter 5

Double Four-Patch

I made my first Double Four-Patch (Fig. 5-1) as an Amish miniature in 1985 or 1986 with Kerry Dunn. The dark and light strips were ½″ instead of 2½″, so this larger version seemed like a piece of cake. Piecing the Double Four-Patch is a great way to learn to match up your seams.

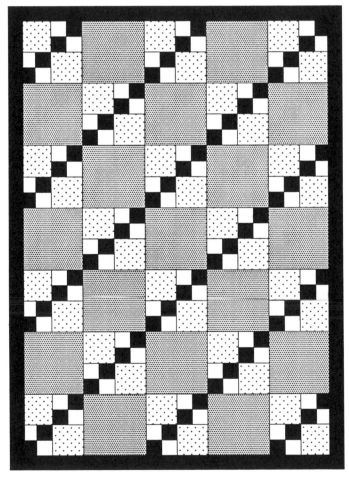

Fig. 5-1

This quilt is beautiful with a Hoffman floral fabric as the background square. The word *background* seems so boring; the name *Hoffman* makes it much more exciting. The Hoffman Fabric Company makes wonderful prints with beautiful colors.

There are several size choices with this quilt. The full and queen have the same number of blocks, just different size borders. The king size has the same borders as the queen but includes two extra rows of blocks. Enjoy!

Slicing

Slice fabrics for your blocks and borders according to the following charts.

Dimensions of Quilts, Double Four-Patch

	Crib	Twin	Full	Queen	King
Finished size	39″ × 51″	68″ × 100″	84″ × 100″	92″ × 108″	108″ × 108″
Size of blocks	6″	8″	8″	8″	8″
Total number of blocks	35	77	99	99	121
Number of pieced blocks	18	39	50	50	61
Number of solid blocks	17	38	49	49	60
Number of blocks across	5	7	9	9	11
Number of blocks down	7	11	11	11	11
Borders (finished size)	1″, 3½″	2″, 4″	2″, 4″	2″, 3″, 5″	2″, 3″, 5″

Fabric Requirements, Double Four-Patch

	Crib	Twin	Full	Queen	King
Light	fat quarter (18″ × 22″)	1¼ yds	1¼ yds	1¼ yds	1½ yds
Medium	½ yd	1¼ yds	1¾ yds	3 yds	3 yds
Dark	1½ yds	2½ yds	2½ yds	2½ yds	3 yds
Background	1½ yds	4 yds	4¾ yds	4¾ yds	5¾ yds

Slicing information for Blocks, Double Four-Patch

Note: Before slicing you will need to tear your background fabric for all sizes except crib as follows: For twin size, tear into two pieces: 108″ and 36″. For full and queen sizes, tear into two pieces: 108″ and 63″. For king size, tear into two pieces: 117″ and 90″.

	Crib	Twin	Full	Queen	King
Dark					
Number of slices	4	5	6	6	6
Size of slices	2″×54″	2½″×90″	2½″×90″	2½″×90″	2½″×108″
Light					
Number of slices	8	10	12	12	12
Size of slices	2″×18″	2½″×45″	2½″×45″	2½″×45″	2½″×54″
Medium					
Number of slices	9	8	9	5	6
Size of slices	3½″×18″	4½″×45″	4½″×63″	4½″×108″	4½″×108″
Background					
Number of slices	3	2	2	2	2
Size of slices	6½″×54″	8½″×108″	×108″	8½″×108″	8½″×117″
Number of slices	—	4	4	4	4
Size of slices	—	8½″×36″	8½″×63″	8½″×63″	8½″×76½″

Slicing Information for Borders and Binding, Double Four-Patch

See note in preceding chart about tearing fabric before slicing.

	Crib	Twin	Full	Queen	King
Dark (border 1)					
Number of border strips	4	4	4	4	4
Size of slices	1½″×54″	2½″×90″	2½″×90″	2½″×90″	2½″×108″
Medium (border 1A)					
Number of border strips	—	—	—	4	4
Size of slices	—	—	—	3½″×108″	3½″×108″
Background (border 2)					
Number of border strips	4	4	4	4	4
Size of slices	4″×54″	4½″×108″	4½″×108″	5½″×108″	5½″×117″
Dark (binding)					
Number of bind strips	4	4	5	5	5
Size of slices	2″×54″	2″×90″	2″×90″	2″×90″	2″×108″

Piecing

1. To start building the small Four-Patches, take your light and dark strips (Fig. 5-2) and place them right sides together. Sew a ¼″ seam down the long side.

2. Lay the sewn strip on the ironing board dark side up. Slide the tip of your iron inside. Open up the strip as you press. You are pressing the right side of the fabric. Press the seam to the dark side. Slice the sewn strips as follows (Fig. 5-3):

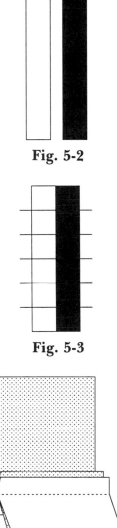

Fig. 5-2

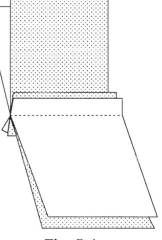

Fig. 5-3

	Crib	Twin	Full	Queen	King
Size of slices	2″	2½″	2½″	2½″	2½″
Number of slices	72	156	200	200	244

3. Now you are going to sew your slices into Four-Patches. Most important at this point is to get an exact intersection—a piece of cake if you approach it from the right direction. First, get out your long needle (see page 16). Take your first slice and place it right side up, light side at the top. Place another slice on top, right side down, dark portion at the top (Fig. 5-4). The seams must lock into place. The top seam goes up toward the needle. As you lock the seams into place, hold down the top seam with your long needle to keep it in place. Sew a ¼″ seam along the side. Continue sewing slices into Four-Patches, stringing them together without clipping the threads, until you have the proper number of Four-Patches (two per block) as follows:

Crib	Twin	Full	Queen	King
36	78	100	100	122

It is faster to sew them all before you cut them apart and look, but you may not be able to wait. Go ahead and peek. If your intersections are not right, let's work on them. You may have under- or overcompensated, trying to get your seam correct. As you hold your slices together, you have to feel that they are exact. You should be able to feel the bump if you have overshot the seam. There will be a gap that your fingers can feel if you haven't locked them tight. Keep trying. Figure 5-5 shows a perfect inter-

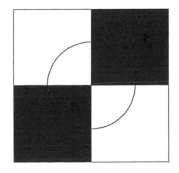

Fig. 5-4

Fig. 5-5

Fig. 5-6

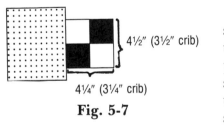

4½" (3½" crib)

4¼" (3¼" crib)

Fig. 5-7

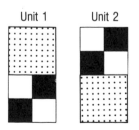

Unit 1   Unit 2

Fig. 5-8

section. There is no right or wrong direction to press your new seam. You do need to be consistent, though; iron them all the same.

4. You are now ready for the next step. Get your medium slices. Place a medium strip right side up on your machine. Lay the Four-Patch blocks right side down. A light square will be in the *upper right-hand corner* (Fig. 5-6). It really *does* make a difference which direction you lay these on your strip. (I won't tell you how many blocks I have made that did not do what I wanted them to do.) Leave a slight (¼") space between blocks. This will allow you to cut the blocks apart easily and to square up later. Sew a ¼" seam. (Why do I keep saying that? That is the only seam allowance I know how to use.)

5. I prefer to cut these squares apart with scissors. I lay them on the table, strip down, blocks on top, seam toward me. I used to do this on my lap, sitting in front of my machine. It was so easy. But I decided the table was safer after I cut into my skirt. Actually the block and strip are too wide to cut accurately in your lap. Another way to do this is to fold the medium strip at the gap between blocks, even up the blocks, then cut the medium with a pair of scissors. Whatever method you choose, cut your blocks apart.

6. Press the seams toward your plain square. It is best to do this from the right side of the fabric. You cannot afford a pleat here. If you lay the block on the ironing board, plain square on top, it will happen like magic. Slip the point of the iron in between the Four-Patch and plain block. The seam will be pressed in the proper direction.

7. Take your pressed blocks (Fig. 5-7) to the cutting board. To square the pairs, lay your ruler on the block with a vertical line of the ruler running along the seam between the Four-Patch and the plain block. Place a horizontal line at 2¼" (crib 1¾") in the middle seam of the Four-Patch. With your rotary cutter, slice off the extra fabric of the plain square. Turn the block 180 degrees and position as before. Use a vertical line to mark the seam between the Four-Patch and plain square, making a horizontal mark at the middle of the Four-Patch. Trim again.

8. Now you will make the Double Four-Patch. Lay out your units in pairs as shown in Fig. 5-8. Place Unit 2 on top of Unit 1, right sides together. Lock your seam together as you did for the first Four-Patch (unless your Four-Patch did not come out perfect, in which case, try again).

9. Sew all of your Four-Patch units into Double Four-Patches. You will have the following number of Double Four-Patch units;

Crib	Twin	Full	Queen	King
18	39	50	50	61

10. The Double Four-Patches will be sewn to your strips of background fabric, which should be 8½" wide (crib 6½"). Lay your strips on the machine right side up. Place your Double Four-Patches on top. There will be a dark in the upper left-hand corner (Fig. 5-9). Sew the following number (not all) of the Four-Patch units to the strips of the background fabric:

	Crib	Twin	Full	Queen	King
	14	33	44	44	55

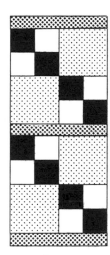

Fig. 5-9

You will have six extra Double Four-Patches (four for the crib size). Take your leftover background strip and cut five 8½" squares (three 6½" squares for the crib).

11. Cut apart the 8½" background strips with the Double Four-Patches sewn on them as before. Be careful as you cut them apart. If you cut crooked, you might shorten one of your blocks. It would not be the end of the world, but. . . .

12. Press the seam toward the background block.

13. Square up this block as you have done before.

14. What you have now are pairs, a pieced and a plain block sewn together. Sew pairs together to form rows, beginning with a pieced block. Now, for all sizes, at the *end* of your *odd* rows sew a Double Four-Patch. At the *beginning* of your *even* rows sew a plain block. Each row now has the following number of blocks across:

	Crib	Twin	Full	Queen	King
	5	7	9	9	11

Press all seams toward the plain square.

15. Sew the rows together, locking your seams so that they go in opposite directions.

16. Now it is time for borders. See page 9, and refer to the border widths at the beginning of this section. Cut the first border (the narrowest) from the length of darkest fabric: Cut two pieces to match the length measurement of the quilt. Pin these borders into place. Sew them on. Press the seams to the outside and square your corners with the rotary cutter. Now measure the width of the quilt. Cut the last two dark strips to that length. Pin and sew on the top and bottom borders. Press these to the outside and square these corners. Repeat for the rest of the borders.

Finishing

After the corners are squared, your top is finished—ready to baste, quilt, and bind. Review Chapter 1 for your options.

Lone Star, by Evelyn Stewart.

Log Cabin, by Beckie Olson, quilted by Juanita Noel, owned by Bill and Lucy Wheeler. *Inset, Bear's Paw doll quilt, by Vickie Jones. Opposite page*, Churn Dash Star in the Window, by Beckie Olson and the quilt group Patches and Pieces, quilted by Juanita Noel.

Opposite: Top, Double Irish Chain, by Adele Lunty. *Bottom*, Single Irish Chain, made for Jennifer Coates by her mother, Deborah Coates. Tied with the Decatur knot, quilted borders.

Above: Left, Reed's Rags, by Susan Day. Tied with the Decatur knot, quilted borders. *Right*, Lone Star wall hanging with scrap border by Kuniko Yamamoto.

Top, Log Cabin (Barn Raising), by Beckie Olson, quilted by Juanita Noel.
Bottom, Sailboat, by Mary Ann Davis.

Top, Double Four-Patch, by Judy Marwil, quilted by Juanita Noel. *Bottom*, Rail Fence, by Suzanne Fain.

Top, School House, by Tomi Shiratori. *Bottom,* Trip Around the World, by Joyce Livesay. Tied with the Decatur knot. Reed's Rags miniature, by Susan Day.

INTERMEDIATE
QUILTS BY THE SLICE

Chapter 6

Double Nine-Patch

This is a classic two-color quilt, with simple and elegant lines (Fig. 6-1). If you are looking for an easy project, but are willing to put in lots of time, this quilt is for you. I used three fabrics for the Double Nine-Patch shown in the color section. In the Fabric Requirements chart, I have listed the light fabric for the small Nine-Patches separately from the fabric for the small and large background squares, but you may combine them if you wish to use only two fabrics.

Fig. 6-1

The lengthwise grain and fiber content of your fabric play an important role in this quilt. Do not substitute a blend or thin cotton for a good-quality cotton in this one.

Slicing

Take your Nine-Patch dark fabric. On the length slice all the strips you need for the blocks, borders, and bindings (see charts). Next slice all the pieces you need for the Nine-Patch light fabric, also on the length. Finally, slice your background fabric.

I like to cut my strips shorter before sewing my units together. Somewhere around 30″ to 36″ long is easier to work with. If you do shorten your lengths, you will still need to use the entire piece. For example, if you are making the crib size, your slices are 54″ long. If you cut those in half, they will be 27″ long, but you will have twice as many to sew. The total inches will still be the same.

Dimensions of Quilts, Double Nine-Patch

	Crib	Twin	Full	Queen	King
Finished size	39″ × 57″	57″ × 93″	75″ × 93″	93″ × 111″	111″ × 111″
Size of blocks	9″	9″	9″	9″	9″
Total number of blocks	15	45	63	99	121
Number of blocks across	3	5	7	9	11
Number of blocks down	5	9	9	11	11
Number of pieced blocks (large Nine-Patches)	8	23	32	50	61
Number of solid blocks	7	22	31	49	60
Number of small Nine-Patches	40	115	160	250	305
Border, finished size	2″, 2″, 2″	2″, 2″, 2″	2″, 2″, 2″	2″, 2″, 2″	2″, 2″, 2″

Fabric Requirements, Double Nine-Patch

	Crib	Twin	Full	Queen	King
Nine-Patch dark	1½ yds	2¾ yds	2¾ yds	3⅓ yds	4¼ yds
Nine-Patch light	1½ yds	2¾ yds	2¾ yds	3⅓ yds	4¼ yds
Background squares, large and small	1 yd	3 yds	3¾ yds	5½ yds	6½ yds

Slicing Information for Blocks, Double Nine-Patch

Note: Before slicing you will need to tear some fabric as follows: For the queen size, tear background fabric into two pieces: 108" and 90". For the king size, tear your dark and light yardages into two pieces: 117" and 36"; tear your background fabric into two pieces: 144" and 90".

	Crib	Twin	Full	Queen	King
Nine-Patch dark					
Number of slices	10	10	15	15	15
Size of slices	1½"×54"	1½"×99"	1½"×99"	1½"×120"	1½"×117"
Number of slices	—	—	—	—	20
Size of slices	—	—	—	—	1½"×36"
Nine-Patch light					
Number of slices	8	8	8	12	14
Size of slices	1½"×54"	1½"×99"	1½"×99"	1½"×120"	1½"×117"
Number of slices	—	—	—	—	10
Size of slices	—	—	—	—	1½"×36"
Background					
Number of slices	3*	2	3*	4	4
Size of slices	9½"×36"	9½"×108"	9½"×135"	9½"×108"	9½"×144"
Number of slices	3*	4	3	1	12
Size of slices	3½"×36"	3½"×108"	3½"×135"	9½"×90"	3½"×90"
Number of slices	—	—	—	9	—
Size of slices	—	—	—	3½"×90"	—

*For the crib and full size you will have extra fabric from which you can get a few more 3½" pieces.

Slicing Information for Borders and Binding, Double Nine-Patch

See note in preceding chart about tearing fabrics before slicing.

	Crib	Twin	Full	Queen	King
Dark Nine-Patch (border)					
Number of border strips	4	4	4	4	4
Size of slices	2½"×54"	2½"×82"	2½"×82"	2½"×105"	2½"×105"
Number of border strips	5	5	5	5	5
Size of slices	2½"×12"	2½"×12"	2½"×12"	2½"×12"	2½"×12"
Light Nine-Patch (border)					
Number of border strips	8	8	8	8	8
Size of slices	2½"×54"	2½"×82"	2½"×82"	2½"×105"	2½"×105"
Number of border strips	4	4	4	4	4
Size of slices	2½"×12"	2½"×12"	2½"×12"	2½"×12"	2½"×12"
Dark Nine-Patch (binding)					
Number of border strips	4	4	4	4	4
Size of slices	2"×54"	2"×90"	2"×90"	2"×117"	2"×117"

Piecing

First, let's make the small Nine-Patches. They are the same for the Single Irish Chain (Chapter 4) only much smaller. Because of the smaller size, the flaws will be more noticeable, so be careful!

1. Before you begin to sew, check your seam gauge. An accurate ¼″ allowance is very important. Now take a dark strip and sew it right sides together to a light strip. Press the seam toward the dark. Make two more of these units. Now you have three separate units, each with one light and one dark.

2. Take two of those units and sew dark strips to the light side (Fig. 6-2). We'll call these A-units.

3. Take the remaining unit and sew a light strip to the dark side (Fig. 6-3). We'll call these B-units.

4. Slice A-units into 1½″ slices (Fig. 6-4).

5. Sew and slice the remaining units until you have:

Fig. 6-2

Fig. 6-3

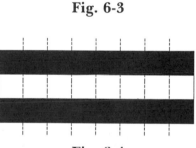

Fig. 6-4

	Crib	Twin	Full	Queen	King
A-unit slices	80	230	320	500	610
B-unit slices	40	115	160	250	305

Now you are ready to have some fun. Place a B-unit slice and an A-unit slice right sides together, with the A-slice on top (Fig. 6-5). Feel the first intersection until it locks into place. After two or three slices you will get the "touch." Sew to the intersection and stop. Keep your long needle on the intersection so it does not move. If you have a "needle down" position on your sewing machine, use it. Otherwise stop and put the needle of your sewing machine down into the intersection. You do not want your fabric slipping on you.

Now get the next intersection ready. There is only 1″ between intersections—not much space to ease. The next seam allowance of the top piece will be pointing toward you and the allowance of piece underneath will be pointing toward the machine. "Feel" it into place and hold it with your long needle. Sew to the edge of that slice. Do not clip your threads; just feed in your next set. (It's OK to peek.) Chain sewing will allow you to have both hands free to piece with, and the machine will always be ready to sew. You don't need to lower the presser foot or hold the thread in the back for a smooth start. Continue until you have used up all of your B-slices. (If you are making a king, you will not be able to stand the wait.)

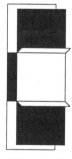

Fig. 6-5

6. Take your pieces and press them toward the A-slice (Row 1). Add Row 3 (an A-slice) in the same way, keeping it on top as you sew. Press toward Row 3.

7. Now let's sew these small Nine-Patches into large Nine-Patches. Take a 3½″-wide slice of the background fabric and place it right side up on the sewing machine. (I used a muslin with no right or wrong side.) Lay your Nine-Patch on top, right side down, with the seams on the Nine-Patch going *across*, not up and down. Leave a scant space between these Nine-Patches as you sew them to the background strip. Do not sew on all of the Nine-Patch blocks:

	Crib	Twin	Full	Queen	King
Leave off	16	46	64	100	122
Sew on	24	69	96	150	183

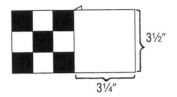

3½"

3¼"

Fig. 6-6

8. Cut between the blocks. Press the seams toward the background square. Trim the background square to the measurements shown on Fig. 6-6.

9. Sew extra pieced blocks onto the background side of these pieces (Fig. 6-7). Make sure the seams of the small Nine-Patch are running *across*, not up and down, as you sew. Make the following number of the units shown in Fig. 6-7:

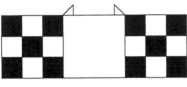

Fig. 6-7

Crib	Twin	Full	Queen	King
16	46	64	100	122

10. Slice the following number of 3½" squares from the remaining 3½" strips of background fabric:

Crib	Twin	Full	Queen	King
8	23	32	50	61

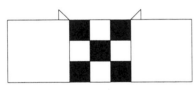

Fig. 6-8

Sew them to the small Nine-Patch side of the remaining units you made in Steps 7 and 8 (Fig. 6-8).

11. Sew the three new rows into a large Nine-Patch the same way you sewed the small Nine-Patches. As you sew the seams, place the units shown in Fig. 6-8 on top (Fig. 6-9). The seam between the small Nine-Patch and the background block will be toward the machine. When you develop a "feel" for matching and sewing the intersections, you can piece any quilt.

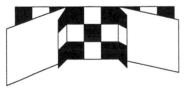

Fig. 6-9

12. After sewing, press the seams toward Row 1 and Row 3 (i.e., away from the middle row). You will make the following number of large Nine-Patch blocks (Fig. 6-10):

Crib	Twin	Full	Queen	King
8	23	32	50	61

13. Now sew the large Nine-Patches to the 9½" background strips. As you sew, be sure the seam lines of the large Nine-Patch run

Fig. 6-10

across, not up and down. Sew the following number of large Nine-Patches onto the strips:

	Crib	Twin	Full	Queen	King
	5	18	27	44	55

14. After you have sewn your blocks onto the strip, cut them apart and press toward the plain block. Trim the plain block to the measurements shown in Fig. 6-11. You will have the following number of large Nine-Patch blocks left over:

	Crib	Twin	Full	Queen	King
	3	5	5	6	6

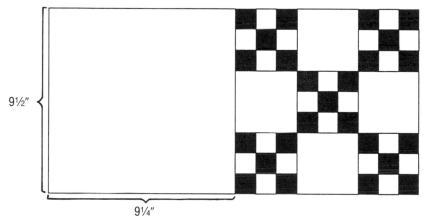

9½"

9¼"

Fig. 6-11

15. From your leftover 9½" background strip slice the following number of additional 9½" squares:

	Crib	Twin	Full	Queen	King
	2	4	4	5	5

16. Sew your pairs into rows, beginning with a pieced block. You will place your extra large Nine-Patch blocks at the *end* of each *odd* row. The extra background square goes at the *beginning* of each *even* row. There will now be:

	Crib	Twin	Full	Queen	King
Blocks in a row	3	5	7	9	11
Number of rows	5	9	9	11	11

17. Sew your rows together.

18. Set aside your border and binding fabric. From the leftovers slice: five dark strips, 2½" × 12" and four light strips, 2½" × 12".

19. Sew these into two dark/light/dark units and one light/dark/light unit. Slice these into 2½″ slices (Fig. 6-12). Sew them together to make four Nine-Patch blocks (Fig. 6-13).

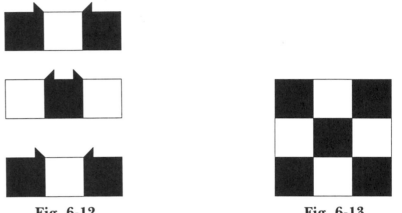

Fig. 6-12   **Fig. 6-13**

20. Measure the center of the quilt from side to side. Then measure the length. Sew one dark border strip between two lights. Press toward the dark. Do this four times. These are your border units.

21. Cut two border units the exact size of the width of the top. Cut the other two the exact size of the length.

22. Pin borders onto the top and bottom of the quilt top, then sew into place. I keep the border on the bottom and the quilt top on top so I can watch and control the pieced seams. Press this seam toward the border.

23. Sew the four Nine-Patches to the ends of the other two borders (Fig. 6-14). Match the intersections and sew these borders on the sides.

Fig. 6-14

Finishing

Now you can move on. This quilt is great in red and muslin or navy and white. Review your options for basting, tying, and quilting in Chapter 1.

Chapter 7

Double Irish Chain

Along with many other patterns featured in this book, the Double Irish Chain falls into the category "Great American Quilt Classics." A two-color quilt with a light background (Fig. 7-1) will give the feeling of an old-time favorite. But you can also make a contemporary-looking quilt by using a dark background. I have included fabric information for a two-color quilt, and, later in the chapter, for a

Fig. 7-1

Solid block

Pieced block

Fig. 7-2

three-color piece. Read the slicing directions carefully before you begin.

I will refer to a "solid" block and a "pieced" block (Fig. 7-2). The solid block is also pieced but has a solid center. Traditionally the four corner pieces of the solid block were appliquéd onto a solid square. For speed in construction, the four corner pieces of the solid block will be pieced by the slice.

You will find this quilt more time-consuming than the Single Irish Chain, but the finished quilt will be worth the extra sewing.

As with any two-block quilt, you will need an odd number of rows and of blocks per row. A row that starts with a pieced block must end with a pieced block. The twin, full, and king quilts are made with a 10″ block. The queen-size quilt and crib quilt use smaller-sized blocks.

Two-Color Double Irish Chain

Slicing

Slice your fabric according to the following charts.

Dimensions of Quilts, Two-Color Double Irish Chain

	Crib	Twin	Full	Queen	King
Finished size	35″ × 45″	67″ × 107″	87″ × 107″	96½″ × 112″	108″ × 108″
Size of blocks	5″	10″	10″	7½″	10″
Total number of blocks	35	45	63	143	81
Number of pieced blocks	18	23	32	72	41
Number of solid blocks	17	22	31	71	40
Number of blocks across	5	5	7	11	9
Number of blocks down	7	9	9	13	9
Borders (finished width)	1″, 1½″, 2½″	2″, 2½″, 4″	2″, 2½″, 4″	1½″, 2″, 3½″	2″, 2½″, 4½″

Fabric Requirements, Two-Color Double Irish Chain

	Crib	Twin	Full	Queen	King
Light (background)	1½ yds	5 yds	6 yds	7¾ yds	7¾ yds
Dark (chain)	1½ yds	5 yds	6 yds	7¾ yds	6½ yds

Slicing Information for Blocks, Two-Color Double Irish Chain

Note: Before slicing, you will need to tear some of your fabric as follows: For the twin size, tear each fabric into two pieces: 3¼ yards (117″) and 1¾ yards (63″). For the full size, tear each fabric into piece 1 and piece 2, each 3 yards (108″). For the queen size, tear each fabric into two pieces: 3½ yards (126″) and 4¼ yards (153″). For the king size, tear light fabric into piece 1 and piece 2, each 3½ yards (117″) and piece 3, 45″. Tear dark fabric into piece 1 and piece 2, each 3¼ yards (117″).

	Crib	Twin	Full	Queen	King
Light (background)					
Number of slices	3	3	3 (from piece 1)	6	3 (from piece 1)
Size of slices	3½″ × 54″	6½″ × 117″	6½″ × 108″	5″ × 126″	6½″ × 117″
Number of slices	12	4	4 (from piece 1)	19	4 (from piece 1)
Size of slices	1½″ × 54″	2½″ × 117″	2½″ × 108″	2″ × 153″	2½″ × 117″
Number of slices	—	13	13 (from piece 2)	—	15 (from piece 2)
Size of slices	—	2½″ × 63″	2½″ × 108″	—	2½″ × 117″
Number of slices	—	—	1 (from picce 2)	—	5 (from piece 3)
Size of slices	—	—	6½″ × 54″	—	6½″ × 45″
Dark (chain)					
Number of slices	9	2	5 (from piece 1)	16	1 (from piece 1)
Size of slices	1½″ × 54″	2½″ × 117″	2½″ × 108″	2″ × 153″	2½″ × 117″
Number of slices	—	12	11 (from piece 2)	—	16 (from piece 2)
Size of slices	—	2½″ × 63″	2½″ × 108″	—	2½″ × 117″

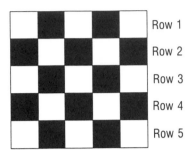

Row 1
Row 2
Row 3
Row 4
Row 5

Fig. 7-3

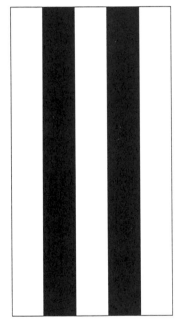

Fig. 7-4

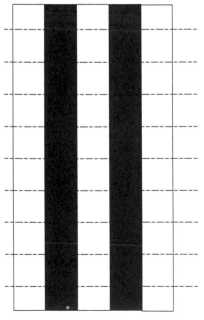

Fig. 7-5

Slicing Information for Borders and Binding, Two-Color Double Irish Chain

See note in preceding chart about tearing some fabrics before slicing.

	Crib	Twin	Full	Queen	King
Inner border (dark)					
Number of border strips	4	4	4 (from piece 1)	4	4 (from piece 1)
Size of slices	1½″ × 54″	2½″ × 117″	2½″ × 108″	2″ × 126″	2½″ × 117″
Middle border (light)					
Number of border strips	4	4	4 (from piece 1)	4	4 (from piece 1)
Size of slices	2″ × 54″	3″ × 117″	3″ × 108″	2½″ × 126″	3″ × 117″
Outer border (dark)					
Number of border strips	4	4	4 (from piece 1)	4	4 (from piece 1)
Size of slices	3″ × 54″	4½″ × 117″	4½″ × 108″	4″ × 126″	5″ × 117″
Binding (dark)					
Number of binding strips	4	4	4 (from piece 2)	4	4 (from piece 1)
Size of slices	2″ × 54″	2″ × 117″	2″ × 108″	2″ × 126″	2″ × 117″

Piecing

1. Start with the pieced block. You will use only your narrow strips for this. There are two types of rows. Rows 1, 3, and 5 are identical, as are Rows 2 and 4 (Fig. 7-3). Using a ¼″ seam, sew your narrower light and dark strips together as shown in Fig. 7-4. (Use the 63″ strips for the twin.) Press seams toward dark as you go. Make this unit twice for crib and twin size, three times for all other sizes. Your unit after sewing should measure this wide:

Crib	Twin	Full	Queen	King
5½″	10½″	10½″	8″	10½″

2. You will now slice it (Fig. 7-5) into pieces this wide:

Crib	Twin	Full	Queen	King
1½″	2½″	2½″	2″	2½″

You will need the following number of slices to complete Rows 1, 3, and 5 of your blocks:

Crib	Twin	Full	Queen	King
54	69	96	216	123

3. To make Rows 2 and 4, sew your narrower light and dark strips together as shown in Fig. 7-6. (Use your 117″ strips for the twin.) As before, use a ¼″ seam and press seam toward the dark. Slice into pieces this wide:

Crib	Twin	Full	Queen	King
1½″	2½″	2½″	2″	2½″

To complete Rows 2 and 4 you will need the following number of slices:

Crib	Twin	Full	Queen	King
36	46	64	144	82

4. Now let's complete the pieced blocks. Sew Row 1 to Row 2 (Fig. 7-7). Row 2 must be on top to lock in the seams. Use your long darning needle to hold down the top seam. As soon as you have sewn over the first intersection, stop and secure the next intersection. You may have to pull your top or bottom piece slightly to get them to match. Hold these intersections in place with your long needle. Sew through that intersection. Continue sewing Rows 1 and 2 together until you have used all your Row 2 slices. You will have the following number of units:

Crib	Twin	Full	Queen	King
36	46	64	144	82

You will have the following number of Row 1 slices left over:

Crib	Twin	Full	Queen	King
18	23	32	72	41

These leftover slices will now become Row 3.

5. Sew all Row 3 slices to Row 1/Row 2 units (Fig. 7-8). To lock in the seams, keep the Row 1/Row 2 unit on top as you sew.

6. Your remaining Row 1/Row 2 units now become Row 4/Row 5 units. Sew these to the three-row units you pieced in Step 5 (Fig. 7-9). You should have the following number of completed pieced blocks:

Crib	Twin	Full	Queen	King
18	23	32	72	41

7. Now let's sew the solid block. Take a length (or lengths) of your light fabric, as follows:

	Crib	Twin	Full	Queen	King
Number of pieces	1	1	1	3	5
Size of pieces	3½″ × 54″	6½″ × 117″	6½″ × 108″ 6½″ × 54″	5″ × 126″	6½″ × 45″

Fig. 7-6

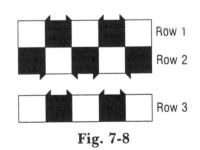

Row 1
Row 2

Fig. 7-7

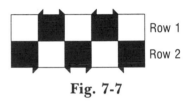

Row 1
Row 2
Row 3

Fig. 7-8

Row 1
Row 2
Row 3

Row 4
Row 5

Fig. 7-9

Sew these pieces between two pieces of dark fabric (Fig. 7-10). The dark pieces will measure:

	Crib	Twin	Full	Queen	King
Number of pieces	2	2	3	6	5
Size of pieces	1½″ × 54″	2½″ × 117″	2½″ × 108″	2″ × 126″	2½″ × 117″

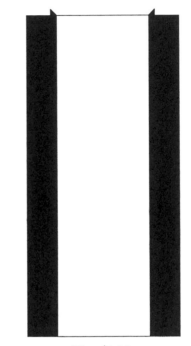

Fig. 7-10

Press toward dark.

8. Slice these units (Fig. 7-11) into the following number of slices:

	Crib	Twin	Full	Queen	King
Number of slices	34	44	62	142	80
Size of slices	1½″	2½″	2½″	2″	2½″

9. Take the remaining wide strips of light fabric, as follows:

	Crib	Twin	Full	Queen	King
Number of pieces	2	2	2	3	3
Size of pieces	3½″ × 54″	6½″ × 117″ 6½″ × 54″	6½″ × 108″	5″ × 126″	6½″ × 117″

On each side of these wider strips, sew strips of light fabric of the following width (Fig. 7-12).

	Crib	Twin	Full	Queen	King
Number of pieces	4	4	4	6	6
Size of pieces	1½″ × 54″	2½″ × 117″ 2½″ × 54″	2½″ × 108″	2″ × 126″	2½″ × 117″

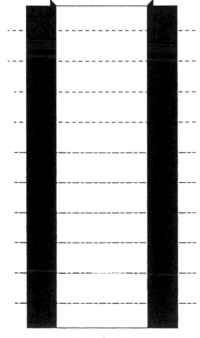

Fig. 7-11

Fig. 7-12

Press these seams toward the center strip.

10. Slice into pieces this wide (Fig. 7-13).

	Crib	Twin	Full	Queen	King
	3½"	6½"	6½"	5"	6½"

Fig. 7-13

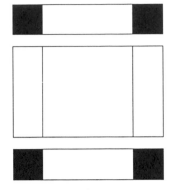

Fig. 7-14

11. Sew the end slices you make in Steps 7 and 8 to your center piece (Fig. 7-14). The center piece must be on the bottom to lock in the seams. To complete your quilt, you will need the following number of solids blocks:

	Crib	Twin	Full	Queen	King
	17	22	31	71	40

12. Press all the new seams toward the center section. At this point turn your blocks over and look at the direction in which the seams have been pressed. Stack your pieced blocks with all of the seams going in the same direction. It is important that the row seams lie horizontally as you sew your pieced block to your solid block. The seams at the corner of a solid block should lock into the seams of the pieced block.

13. Sew your blocks into rows. The odd rows start and end with a pieced block, while the even rows start and end with a solid block. You will have the following number of blocks per row:

	Crib	Twin	Full	Queen	King
	5	5	7	11	9

and the following number of rows:

	Crib	Twin	Full	Queen	King
	7	9	9	13	9

As you sew your rows together, be sure to lock the seams together.

14. After you sew the rows together, it is time for borders. First take borders from your dark fabric. Set aside the strips designated as binding. You will not need the binding until after you finish the quilting. The border strips are all too long; you will need to cut them to fit. First, carefully measure the length of the quilt through the center and then at the edges as discussed on page 9. If the edge of your quilt top measurement is not the same as the center, check and correct the problem at this point. You don't want your quilt to have wavy edges. Take two pieces of the narrow border from your dark fabric. They should measure the length of your top. Sew these two pieces on the long sides of the quilt. Press away from the top. Take the remaining two pieces of narrow dark fabric and sew one on the top and one on the bottom. Press, then check to see if the corners are square.

15. Next sew on the middle border (this was cut from your light fabric). Sew on the two long sides first. Press toward dark, then sew on top and bottom pieces.

16. The final border is a wide border of dark fabric. Sew on the two long sides, then the top and bottom.

Finishing

You are now ready to baste your quilt. Review Chapter 1 for your options on quilting or tying.

Three-Color Double Irish Chain

I made this a separate section because the fabric requirements are different from the requirements for the traditional two-color Double Irish Chain. In these instructions, I've used light for the background, dark for the chain, and medium for the inner chain (Fig. 7-15), but you can experiment with colors and patterns for different effects.

Fig. 7-15

Slicing

Dimensions of Quilts, Three-Color Double Irish Chain

	Crib	Twin	Full	Queen	King
Finished size	40″ × 50″	67″ × 107″	87″ × 107″	95″ × 112″	108″ × 108″
Size of blocks	5″	10″	10″	7½″	10″
Total number of blocks	35	45	63	143	81
Number of pieced blocks	18	23	32	72	41
Number of solid blocks	17	22	21	71	40
Number of blocks across	5	5	7	11	9
Number of blocks down	7	9	9	13	9
Borders (finished size)	2″, 2½″, 3″	2″, 2½″, 4″	2″, 2½″, 4″	1″, 2″, 3½″	2″, 2½″, 4½″

Fabric Requirements, Three-Color Double Irish Chain

	Crib	Twin	Full	Queen	King
Light (background)	1½ yds	4 yds	4¼ yds	5½ yds	6½ yds
Dark (chain)	1½ yds	4 yds	4¼ yds	5½ yds	6½ yds
Medium (inner chain)	1 yd	1⅔ yds	2¾ yds	2¾ yds	3¼ yds

Slicing Information for Blocks, Three-Color Double Irish Chain

Note: Before slicing, you will need to tear some fabrics as follows: For the twin size, tear dark (chain) fabric into two pieces: 117″ and 27″. For the full size, tear light (background) and dark (chain) fabrics into two pieces: 3 yards (108″) and 1¼ yards (45″). For the queen size, tear light (background) and dark (chain) fabrics into two pieces: 3¼ yards (117″) and 2¼ yards (81″). For the king size, tear light and dark fabrics into two pieces, each 3¼ yards (117″).

	Crib	Twin	Full	Queen	King
Light (background)					
Number of slices	3	2	3	3	5 (from piece 1)
Size of slices	3½″ × 54″	6½″ × 117″	6½″ × 108″	5″ × 117″	6½″ × 117″
Number of slices	7	6	8	6	3 (from piece 1)
Size of slices	1½″ × 54″	2½″ × 117″	2½″ × 45″	2″ × 117″	2½″ × 117″

	Crib	Twin	Full	Queen	King
Number of slices	—	1	4	8	7 (from piece 2)
Size of slices	—	6½″ × 27″	2½″ × 108″	2″ × 81″	2½″ × 117″
Dark (chain) Number of slices	9	9	8*	8	16 (from piece 1)
Size of slices	1½″ × 54″	2½″ × 117″	2½″ × 108″	2″ × 117″	2½″ × 117″
Number of slices	—	—	12	20	—
Size of slices	—	—	2½″ × 45″	2″ × 81″	—
Medium (inner chain) Number of slices	10	9	9‡	18	9
Size of slices	1½″ × 27″	2½″ × 60″	2½″ × 90″	2″ × 81″	2½″ × 117″

* Cut six of the 2½″ × 108″ strips into 45″ lengths.
‡ Cut these nine strips to 2½″ × 45″.

Slicing Information for Borders and Binding, Three-Color Double Irish Chain

See note on preceding chart about tearing some fabrics before slicing.

	Crib	Twin	Full	Queen	King
Medium (inner border) Number of border strips	4	6	4	4	4
Size of slices	2½″ × 36″	2½″ × 60″	2½″ × 99″	1½″ × 99″	2½″ × 117″
Light (middle border) Number of border strips	4	4	4	4	4 (from piece 2)
Size of slices	3″ × 54″	3″ × 117″	3″ × 108″	2½″ × 117″	3″ × 117″
Dark (outer border) Number of border strips	4	4	4	4	4 (from piece 2)
Size of slices	3½″ × 54″	4½″ × 117″	4½″ × 108″	4″ × 117″	5″ × 117″
Dark (binding) Number of border strips	4	14	—	4	4 (from piece 2)
Size of slices	2″ × 54″	2″ × 27″	—	2″ × 117″	2″ × 117″
Medium (binding) Number of slices	—	—	4	—	—
Size of slices	—	—	2″ × 99″	—	—

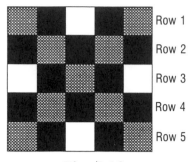

Row 1
Row 2
Row 3
Row 4
Row 5

Fig. 7-16

Piecing

For the three-color quilt, follow the Piecing directions beginning on page 62 for the Two-Color quilts, *except* your pieced block for a three-color Double Irish Chain will have three kinds of units to set together (Fig. 7-16):

✳ Rows 1 and 5 are identical. Piece your strips as shown in Fig. 7-17, then slice.

Fig. 7-17

✳ Rows 2 and 4 are identical. Piece your strips as shown in Fig. 7-18, then slice.

✳ For Row 3, piece your strips as shown in Fig. 7-19, then slice.

Fig. 7-18

Fig. 7-19

The solid block is constructed exactly the same as for the Double Irish Chain, page 62–64.

Chapter 8

Reed's Rags

Reed's Rags was named after my friend Pat Reed. She had made a few Quilts by the Slice and had some 2½″ strips left over. She made Four-Patches out of them and set them together to make what she considered to be a scrap or rag quilt (Fig. 8-1). Oh, what beautiful rags! I modified the piecing, using new, long strips, rather than leftovers, and incorporated it into my class schedule.

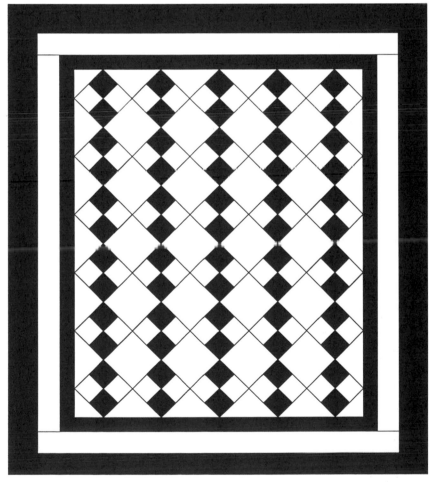

Fig. 8-1

My quilt group, Patches and Pieces, also made this quilt. The eight of us meet for three hours, one night a week. Each of us wanted to make a full-sized quilt, but we also wanted to share blocks with some members of the group who had moved away. We therefore needed enough blocks for ten quilts—a total of 1,800 Four-Patches.

One evening we brought along some fabric from our stashes. Among us, we had a super selection. Some members were a little selfish at first, but we talked them into throwing their cherished fabric into the pot.

We separated our fat quarters into two piles, one containing 70 lights and the other, 70 darks. We ironed and sliced our fat quarters on the length into 2½″ × 18″ strips. That gave us 560 strips of light and 560 strips of dark. The next week we met again. Three of us sewed strips together, two pressed, one sliced, and two assembled Four-Patches. We decided that, if possible, we would each get one of each combination. The patches that we as individuals didn't like would go into our "pillow tucks." Now that we were excited, we all brought more fabric to go into our "rag" quilt. More fabric was sliced, more Four-Patches made.

Our third meeting was spent doing the same tasks as the second. The Four-Patches were completed that night. At that point we fell apart. Progress depended on us actually washing and slicing our muslin. Some nights we did more snacking than sewing. We finally finished the tops. Some quilts were tied, others quilted. Some are still in progress. After all, it has been only four years, and we had more than 2,000 Four-Patches!

Slicing

Slice all of your fat quarters with your 2½″ plastic strip or ruler into slices measuring 2½″ × 18″. You should get eight slices per piece of fabric.

Slice the muslin into 4½″ strips and 5″ strips (see charts).

Dimensions of Quilts, Reed's Rags

	Crib	Twin	Full	Queen	King
Finished size	40½″ × 46″	68½″ × 95½″	86″ × 102″	91½″ × 108″	108″ × 108″
Size of blocks	4″	4″	4″	4″	4″
Total number of blocks	50	230	334	388	481
Number of pieced blocks	30	126	180	208	256
Number of solid blocks	20	104	154	180	225
Number of side triangles	18 + 4 corners	42 + 4 corners	50 + 4 corners	54 + 4 corners	60 + 4 corners
Number of blocks across	5	9	12	13	16

	Crib	Twin	Full	Queen	King
Number of blocks down	6	14	15	16	16
Borders (finished size)	1½", 2", 3"	2", 3", 4½"	2", 3", 5"	2", 3", 5"	2", 3", 5"

Fabric Requirements, Reed's Rags

	Crib	Twin	Full	Queen	King
Number of light fat quarters (18" × 22")	2*	5	6	8	10
Number of dark fat quarters (18" × 22")	2*	5	6	8	10
Muslin	1½ yds	4 yds	4½ yds	4¾ yds	5¾ yds
Dark (for borders)	1½ yds	3 yds	3 yds	3¼ yds	3¼ yds

*You might want to use scraps for variety.

Slicing Information for Blocks, Reed's Rags

Note: Before slicing, you will need to tear some fabric as follows: For the twin size, tear muslin into two pieces: 108" and 36". For the full size, tear muslin into two pieces: 108" and 54". For the queen size, tear muslin into two pieces: 117" and 54". For the king size, tear muslin into two pieces: 117" and 90"

	Crib	Twin	Full	Queen	King
Light fat quarters					
Number of slices	16	40	48	64	80
Size of slices	2½" × 18"	2½" × 18"	2½" × 18"	2½" × 18"	2½" × 18"
Dark fat quarters					
Number of slices	16	40	48	64	80
Size of slices	2½" × 18"	2½" × 18"	2½" × 18"	2½" × 18"	2½" × 18"
Muslin					
Number of slices	1*	4*	2*	2*	2*
Size of slices	5" × 54"	5" × 36"	5" × 108"	5" × 117"	5" × 90"
Number of slices	2	5	4	4	6
Size of slices	4½" × 54"	4½" × 108"	4½" × 108"	4½" × 117"	4½" × 90"
Number of slices	—	—	7	9	6
Size of slices	—	—	4½" × 54"	4½" × 54"	4½" × 117"

*Cut these 5" slices into squares. Cut in half on the diagonal to make triangles.

Slicing Information for Borders and Binding, Reed's Rags

See note in preceding chart about tearing some fabrics before slicing.

	Crib	Twin	Full	Queen	King
Dark (inner border)					
Number of slices	4	4	4	4	4
Size of slices	2″×54″	2½″×108″	2½″×108″	2½″×117″	2½″×117″
Muslin (middle border)					
Number of slices	4	4	4	4	4
Size of slices	2½″×54″	3½″×108″	3½″×108″	3½″×117″	3½″×117″
Dark (outer border)					
Number of slices	4	4	4	4	4
Size of slices	3½″×54″	5″×108″	5½″×108″	5½″×117″	5½″×117″
Dark (binding)					
Number of slices	4	4	4	4	4
Size of slices	2″×54″	2″×108″	2″×108″	2″×117″	2″×117″

Piecing

Fig. 8-2

1. Start by sewing your light strips to dark strips (Fig. 8-2). Use ¼″ seam. Make a variety of combinations, at least two units of each combination.

2. Press toward the dark. Make sure you do not have a tuck in the seam. It must be fully extended.

3. Slice these units into 2½″ slices (Fig. 8-3). There will be seven slices for each strip.

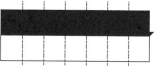

Fig. 8-3

4. Sew slices that match into Four-Patches (Fig. 8-4). You will need the following number of Four-Patches:

Crib	Twin	Full	Queen	King
30	126	180	208	256

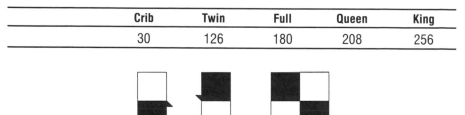

Fig. 8-4

5. Lay out the blocks so that the shorter seams (made in Step 1) run lengthwise. Place a 4½″ muslin strip on the machine. Place the Four-Patches on it, right sides down. A dark square should be in the upper right corner. Sew the blocks to the strip, leaving a scant ¼″ space between blocks (Fig. 8-5).

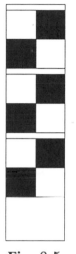

Fig. 8-5

6. Cut between the blocks. Press toward the muslin. Now you have Four-Patch pairs (Fig. 8-6).

7. Lay these out and scramble them up. Lay them out again in diagonal rows. Now step back to look at them. You may be surprised. After you have decided on your layout, sew the Four-Patch pairs to each other in rows.

8. Cut a 5″ strip of muslin into squares. Cut in half on the diagonal to make triangles. Sew these to the ends of rows.

9. Sew on corners.

10. Sew rows together. The top left-hand corner should look like Fig. 8-7.

11. Using a long stitch (6–7 spi), machine-stitch about ¼″ from the edge around the entire quilt top to prevent stretching. Lots of bias!

12. Now sew on borders. Have you ever mitered a border before? It is really very easy. Be very careful measuring for your first border (narrow dark). The blocks have been sewn on point so the edges of the top are bias and could stretch. Measure the length through the center of the top. Divide the measurement in half.

At this point I sew my borders together. (See Figs. 1-13 through 1-16 and the accompanying instructions in Chapter 1.) *Do not* cut your borders the length that your top measured. We will miter these corners. Find the center of the border strips. Take one of the borders and place a pin at the center of the length on the narrow dark side. Place matching pins where half the length of the quilt top is. Carefully sew the two long sides on,

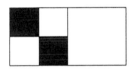

Fig. 8-6

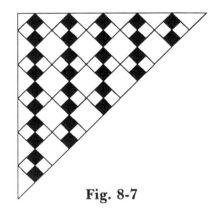

Fig. 8-7

starting ¼″ down from the corner of the top, and stopping ¼″ from the bottom edge.

13. Sew the top and bottom inner borders in the same manner.

14. Lay a corner on the ironing pad. Press one border length out straight. Roll the other to a 45° angle. Match up your light and dark borders.

15. Press, pin into place, and sew. I sew my corners down on the top surface (right side) by hand. My partner, Mary Charles, sews from the bottom or wrong side of the fabric by machine. They are perfect 99% of the time.

16. Repeat for all corners.

Finishing

After you baste this, you are ready to quilt! Review Chapter 1 for tying and quilting options.

Chapter 9

Trip around the World

Traditionally, Trip around the World quilts were made by the Amish, members of a religious community that originally settled in Pennsylvania. Most Trip around the World quilts are made in the Sunshine and Shadows color scheme (Fig. 9-1). The colors blend from light to dark and back again in a bold array of solid fabrics— hence the name Sunshine and Shadows.

Fig. 9-1

The quilt is made up of rows of squares sewn together in a way that allows the pattern and colors of the fabrics to dominate the design. A Trip around the World can be made with any number of fabrics. For ease of design and assembly, these instructions are for six fabrics. You will spend the morning sewing strips together, and after lunch you will see your quilt come to life. After you have made this one, try another by the slice method, but this time use eight or ten fabrics. Remember, your fabric colors and patterns should flow from one piece to the next.

Slicing

Slice your fabric using a 3″ strip for crib size, 3½″ for twin, full, and queen size, or 4½″ for king size. (In the piecing directions that follow, crib and king measurements are given in parentheses.) Cut on the lengthwise grain.

Dimensions of Quilts, Trip around the World

	Crib	Twin	Full	Queen	King
Finished size	39″ × 54″	67″ × 91″	79″ × 97″	95″ × 107″	108″ × 108″
Size of blocks	2½″	3″	3″	3″	4″
Total number of blocks	247	513	667	837	625
Number of blocks across	13	19	23	27	25
Number of blocks down	19	27	29	31	25
Borders (finished size)	3″	2″, 3″	2″, 3″	3″, 4″	4″

Fabric Requirements, Trip around the World

	Crib	Twin	Full	Queen	King
Fabric 1	¾ yd	1½ yds	1⅔ yds	2 yds	2 yds
Fabric 2 (border yardage included)	¾ yd	3 yds	3⅓ yds	4 yds	2 yds
Fabric 3	¾ yd	1½ yds	1⅔ yds	2 yds	2 yds
Fabric 4	¾ yd	1½ yds	1⅔ yds	2 yds	2 yds
Fabric 5	¾ yd	1½ yds	1⅔ yds	2 yds	2 yds
Fabric 6 (border yardage included)	1½ yds	3 yds	3⅓ yds	4 yds	4 yds

Slicing Information for Blocks, Trip around the World

	Crib	Twin	Full	Queen	King
Fabric 1					
Number of slices	7	7	7	7	7
Size of slices	3″ × 27″	3½″ × 54″	3½″ × 60″	3½″ × 72″	4½″ × 72″
Fabric 2					
Number of slices	7	4	4	4	7
Size of slices	3″ × 27″	3½″ × 108″	3½″ × 120″	3½″ × 144″	4½″ × 72″
Fabric 3					
Number of slices	7	7	7	7	7
Size of slices	3″ × 27″	3½″ × 54″	3½″ × 60″	3½″ × 72″	4½″ × 72″
Fabric 4					
Number of slices	7	7	7	7	7
Size of slices	3″ × 27″	3½″ × 54″	3½″ × 60″	3½″ × 72″	4½″ × 72″
Fabric 5					
Number of slices	7	7	7	7	7
Size of slices	3″ × 27″	3½″ × 54″	3½″ × 60″	3½″ × 72″	4½″ × 72″
Fabric 6					
Number of slices	4	4	4	4	4
Size of slices	3″ × 54″	3½″ × 108″	3½″ × 120″	3½″ × 144″	4½″ × 144″

Slicing Information for Borders and Binding, Trip around the World

	Crib	Twin	Full	Queen	King
Fabric 2					
Number of slices	—	4	4	4	—
Size of slices	—	2½″ × 108″	2½″ × 100″	3½″ × 112″	—
Fabric 6					
Number of slices	4	4	4	4	4
Size of slices	3½″ × 54″	3½″ × 108″	3½″ × 108″	4½″ × 112″	4½″ × 110″
Binding (Fabric 6)					
Number of slices	4	4	4	4	13
Size of slices	2″ × 54″	2″ × 108″	2″ × 108″	2″ × 112″	2″ × 34″

Piecing

This is the most time-consuming part of the quilt, but you will know it was worth the effort when you see the results.

1. You will make six panels. Lay your fabric in front of you in six stacks, starting with Fabric 1 at the left (Fig. 9-2). For all sizes

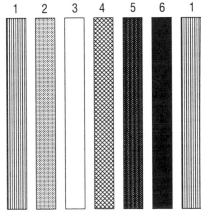

Fig. 9-2

but the crib, cut the four strips of Fabric 5 and 6 in half to make eight strips each 3½″ wide (3″ crib, 4½″ king). Put one of each of these eight strips aside; you will not need it.

2. Take one strip of Fabric 1 and lay it right side up on your machine. Lay one strip of Fabric 2 right side down on top of Fabric 1. Sew a ¼″ seam down the length. Do not clip the threads after sewing the two strips together. Next, feed in one piece of Fabric 2 right side up with a Fabric 3 right side down on top. Sew those together. Remember, do not cut the thread. Just continued to feed in the next pair: Fabrics 3 and 4, then Fabrics 4 and 5, Fabrics 5 and 6, and finally Fabrics 6 and 1. After sewing Fabrics 6 and 1, remove the chain of fabrics from the machine. Do not press.

3. Open up the first panel and sew a Fabric 3 strip onto Fabric 2. In the next panel, sew a Fabric 4 strip on Fabric 3. Continue in this manner. When you get to the last panel, sew a Fabric 2 strip onto a Fabric 1 strip. Remove the chain of fabrics and go back to first panel. Sew Fabric 4 onto Fabric 3 on that panel. Work until you have completed six panels as follows:

Panel 1 (with marker)	1 2 3 4 5 6 1
Panel 2	2 3 4 5 6 1 2
Panel 3	3 4 5 6 1 2 3
Panel 4	4 5 6 1 2 3 4
Panel 5	5 6 1 2 3 4 5
Panel 6	6 1 2 3 4 5 6

Note that each panel starts and ends with the same fabric. Figs. 9-3 through 9-8 show Panels 1 through 6.

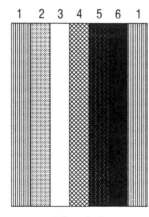

Fig. 9-3

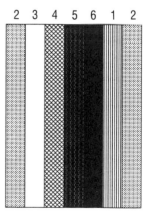

Fig. 9-4

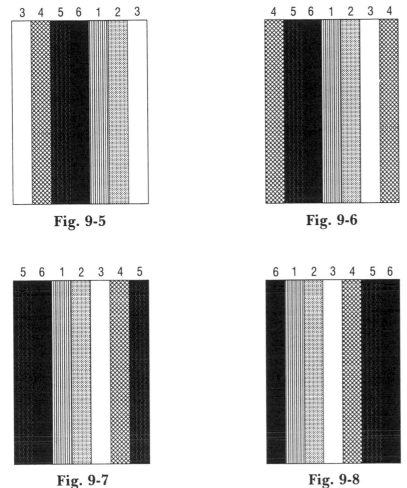

Fig. 9-5

Fig. 9-6

Fig. 9-7

Fig. 9-8

4. Do not press these panels: you need your seams to be movable. Slice each panel into 3½″ slices (3″ for crib, 4½″ for king). Keep your slices straight. The vertical lines on your ruler should run parallel to the seams of your strip unit. If a strip looks crooked, you may have to start over, slicing it slightly bigger and trimming it. Stack your slices near your machine by panel. On a piece of paper copy the number of your first row according to the size of your quilt. The center square is in **boldface** in the following charts:

Crib	3 4 5 6 1 2 **3** 2 1 6 5 4 3
Twin	1 2 3 4 5 6 1 2 3 **4** 3 2 1 6 5 4 3 2 1
Full	5 6 1 2 3 4 5 6 1 2 3 **4** 3 2 1 6 5 4 3 2 1 6 5
Queen	2 3 4 5 6 1 2 3 4 5 6 1 2 **3** 2 1 6 5 4 3 2 1 6 5 4 3 2
King	6 1 2 3 4 5 6 1 2 3 4 5 **6** 5 4 3 2 1 6 5 4 3 2 1 6

5. Now the fun begins! Take a slice from the panels you cut in Step 4, starting with the leftmost number in the chart immediately above. Lay this slice right side up, the fabrics moving from left to right in ascending order—for example, 1 2 3 4 5 6 1 for the twin. Place a pin in the left-hand corner as your marker.

6. Next pick up the slice starting with the next fabric of the rotation, except for the crib, for which add one Panel 2 in *descending* order.

Crib	3	4	5	6	1	2	**3**/2	1	6	5	4	3*	2
Twin	1	2	3	4	5	6	1/2	3	**4***	5	6	1	2
Full	5	6	1	2	3	4	5/6	1	2	3	**4***	5	6
Queen	2	3	4	5	6	1	2/3	4	5	6	1	2	**3**
King	6	1	2	3	4	5	6/1	2	3	4	5	6	

With a long darning needle, pick out the seam following the center square (except for crib size). Rip out as follows (marked by asterisk in chart above):

Crib	Rip out between 3 and 2 in the second slice to complete Row 1
Twin	Rip out between 4 and 5 in the second slice
Full	Rip out between 4 and 5 in the second slice
Queen	Do not rip out
King	Rip out between 6 and 1 in the second slice

Start a "partial pile" from the leftover portions of the slices you ripped out.

7. Now pick up a slice that begins with the fabric number *preceding* the center. Lay it so the fabrics are in *descending* order:

Crib	First row already complete																		
Twin	1	2	3	4	5	6	1	2	3	**4**/3	2	1	6	5	4	3			
Full	5	6	1	2	3	4	5	6	1	2	3	**4**/3	2	1	6	5	4	3	
Queen	2	3	4	5	6	1	2	3	4	5	6	1	2	**3**/2	1	6	5	4	3	2
King	6	1	2	3	4	5	6	1	2	3	4	5	**6**/5	4	3	2	1	6	5

8. To finish the row, pick up the slice with the next fabric in descending order. Sew enough squares on to make the row symmetrical on both sides of the center. (This may be in your partial pile.) Sew this on. Take your darning needle and remove the excess part of the slice.

Crib	already complete
Twin	1 2 3 4 5 6 1 2 3 **4** 3 2 1 6 5 4 3/2 1
	(2 squares)
Full	5 6 1 2 3 4 5 6 1 2 3 **4** 3 2 1 6 5 4 3/2 1 6 5
	(4 squares)
Queen	2 3 4 5 6 1 2 3 4 5 6 1 2 **3** 2 1 6 5 4 3 2/1 6 5 4 3 2
	(6 squares)
King	6 1 2 3 4 5 6 1 2 3 4 5 **6** 5 4 3 2 1 6 5/4 3 2 1 6
	(5 squares)

Row 1 is now complete. Lay it across your lap. There should be a pin in the left-hand block. Leave it and put a pin in the center block.

9. Start Row 2 with the second fabric of Row 1:

Crib	4 5 6 1 2 3 **4**	Sew to	3 2 1 6 5 4 3
Twin	2 3 4 5 6 1 2	Sew to	3 4 **5**
Full	6 1 2 3 4 5 6	Sew to	1 2 3 4 **5**
Queen	3 4 5 6 1 2 3	Sew to	4 5 6 1 2 3 **4**
King	1 2 3 4 5 6 1	Sew to	2 3 4 5 6 **1** 2

Complete the row as you did the first. Press the seams of Row 1 toward the left-hand block that has the pin in it. Press Row 2 in the opposite direction.

10. Now you will sew Row 1 to Row 2. Lay Row 1 on the machine right side up. Lay Row 2 on top right side down. All of the seams on Row 1 will point up, while those on Row 2 will point down. Do not use pins. As you sew, you must feel one seam locking into another. This is one of the most important factors in the construction of this quilt. The long darning needle is perfect for holding that top seam in place. Sew the seam. After sewing, press your row seam toward Row 1.

11. Lay the piece with the pin in the upper left-hand corner at the left. It will stay that way until you are finished. Move the pin from the center block top row to the center block second row. This pin will move down at each row, always marking the center. After a while you will not need the pin in the center.

12. Piece the third row, starting with the next fabric in rotation (the second fabric of Row 2). Press the seams toward the left if looking at the front. All odd rows will be pressed toward the left, even rows toward the right. Place the first two rows on the machine right side up. Lay the third row on top right side down. Since the seams on the bottom go up, the seams on the top will go down. Press the row seams toward Row 1 every time you attach a row.

13. Continue as above for the following number of rows:

Crib	Twin	Full	Queen	King
10	14	15	16	13

The last row you seamed is your center row.

14. Now you will work in descending order to start each row. This row is the same as the row before the center. You will work back until you have the following number of rows:

Crib	Twin	Full	Queen	King
19	27	29	31	25

15. The last row will be the same as the first. Sew your narrowest border on a long side first. It is good to measure the center of your quilt as described on page 9. Cut the lengthwise borders that long. Press with seam toward the border. Square off the corners then sew on the top and bottom borders. Do the same with the last border (crib and king sizes have only one border).

Finishing

You are ready to quilt or tie. Review your options for basting, tying, and quilting in Chapter 1. This is a wonderful pattern on which to try the Decatur knot (see pages 12–13). I usually put in an Extra Loft batting by Fairfield. It ties up very fast and the fibers stay in place. It is best to use a floor frame or a large Q-Snap frame. You are moving so quickly that a lap frame would need to be changed too frequently. The king size takes less than 40 hours to piece, tie, and bind.

By tying this quilt, you can finish it and move on to your next project. Personally I do not wait to tie or quilt a piece before I jump to the next top. As soon as the last border is on, it's back to the drawing board.

Chapter 10

Churn Dash

A churn dash was a kitchen tool used by pioneer women, who named a quilt pattern after it. The Amish also made quilts in the Churn Dash pattern, but set it on point and called it Hole in the Barn Door (another name taken from everyday farm life).

This Churn Dash quilt (Fig. 10-1) is made by using Barbara Johannah's quick triangles and my slice techniques. After making Churn Dash by the slice, try setting it on point for Hole in the Barn Door.

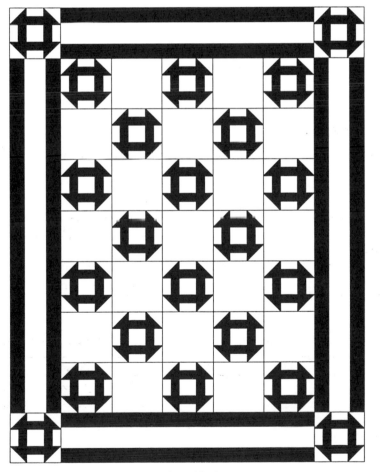

Fig. 10-1

I also used the slice method to make Star in the Window, a Churn Dash with an eight-pointed star in the center. My quilt group, Patches and Pieces, made the eight-pointed stars for me. The Star in the Window pattern was shown in *Quilter's Newsletter* #97.

Slicing

Note: Before you begin slicing, you will need to draw a cutting diagram for each fabric. See Chapter 1, page 4.

Dimensions of Quilts, Churn Dash

	Crib	Twin	Full	Queen	King
Finished size	42″ × 54″	72″ × 96″	75″ × 93″	96″ × 120″	120″ × 120″
Size of blocks	6″	12″	9″	12″	12″
Total number of blocks	39	39	67	67	85
Number of pieced blocks	22	22	36	36	45
Number of solid blocks	17	17	31	31	40
Number of blocks across	5	5	7	7	9
Number of blocks down	7	7	9	9	9
Borders (finished size)	2″, 2″, 2″	2″, 2″, 2″	2″, 2″, 2″	2″, 2″, 2″	2″, 2″, 2″

Fabric Requirements, Churn Dash

	Crib	Twin	Full	Queen	King
Light (background)	2 yds	5 yds	5 yds	8½ yds	10¾ yds
Dark (dash)	1⅝ yds	4 yds	4 yds	6¾ yds	6 yds

Grid Requirements for Half-Square Triangles, Churn Dash

	Crib	Twin	Full	Queen	King
Grid size	15″ × 15″ 5 sq. × 5 sq.	16″ × 20″ 3 sq. × 4 sq.	16″ × 20″ 4 sq. × 5 sq.	15″ × 20″ 3 sq. × 4 sq.	15″ × 20″ 3 sq. × 4 sq.
Number of grid sheets	2	4	4	6	8
Size of squares	2⅞″	4⅞″	3⅞″	4⅞″	4⅞″
Number of half-square triangle units needed	88	88	144	144	180

Crib

Light (2 yards)
2 pieces for grid sheets 15″×15″
17 squares 6½″
1 piece for centers 2½″×56″
4 pieces 1½″×56″
4 border pieces 2½″×56″

Dark (1⅝ yards)
2 pieces for grid sheets 15″×15″
4 pieces 1½″×56″
8 border pieces 2½″×56″
4 binding pieces 2″×56″

Twin

Light (5 yards)
4 pieces for grid sheets 16″×20″
17 squares 12½″
1 piece for centers 4½″×104″
4 pieces 2½″×104″
4 border pieces 2½″×86″

Dark (4 yards)
4 pieces for grid sheets 16″×20″
4 pieces 2½″×104″
8 border pieces 2½″×104″
4 binding pieces 2″×104″

Full

Light (5 yards)
4 pieces for grid sheets 16″×20″
31 squares 9½″
1 piece for centers 3½″×126″
4 pieces 2″×126″
4 border pieces 2½″×126″

Dark (4 yards)
4 pieces for grid sheets 16″×20″
4 pieces 2″×126″
8 border pieces 2½″×104″
4 binding pieces 2″×104″

Queen

Light (8½ yards)
6 pieces for grid sheets 15″×20″
31 squares 12½″
1 piece for centers 4½″×162″, cut
  into 3 pieces 4½″×54″
4 pieces 2½″×112″
2 pieces 2½″×162″, each cut into
  3 pieces 2½″×54″
4 border pieces 2½″×112″

Dark (5¾ yards)
6 pieces for grid sheets 15″×20″
6 pieces 2½″×54″
4 pieces 2½″×112″
8 border pieces 2½″×112″
4 binding pieces 2″×112″

King

Light (10¾ yards)
8 pieces for grid sheets 15″×20″
40 squares 12½″
2 pieces centers 4½″×108″
8 pieces 2½″×108″
2 border pieces 2½″×108″
2 border pieces 2½″×112″

Dark (6 yards)
8 pieces for grid sheets 15″×20″
2 pieces centers 4½″×112″
8 pieces 2½″×108″
8 border pieces 2½″×112″
10 binding pieces 2″×60″

Piecing

1. We will start by quick piecing the triangles. See the chart, Grid Requirements for Half-Square Triangles, Churn Dash. Take

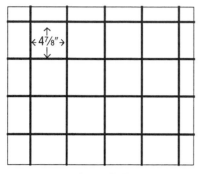

Fig. 10-2

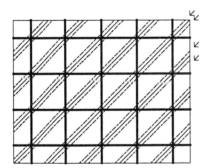

Fig. 10-3

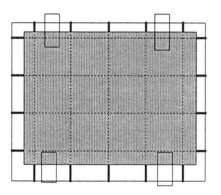

Fig. 10-4

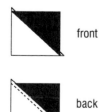

Fig. 10-5

a sheet of graph paper, 17″×22″ (8 squares to the inch.) Carefully draw a grid on it with lines at these intervals:

Crib	Twin	Full	Queen	King
2⅞″	4⅞″	3⅞″	4⅞″	4⅞″

and with this many whole squares:

Crib	Twin	Full	Queen	King
25	12	20	12	12

Use a straightedge to extend these lines to the edge of the paper. Figure 10-2 shows the twin, queen, or king.

2. Take a piece of light fabric the following size:

Crib	Twin	Full	Queen	King
15″×15″	16″×20″	16″×20″	15″×20″	15″×20″

Lay this piece right side down on the grid paper. Transfer the lines from the paper to the fabric (Fig. 10-3). An easy way to do this is to use a long straightedge. Lay it on top of the fabric and line it up with the outside lines on your paper. You may want to tape your fabric with a few pieces of tape to the paper.

3. After you have transferred the lines, draw a diagonal line with a Quilt-N-Sew ruler through each square. Eventually, these will be your cutting lines.

4. Use the Quilt-N-Sew or C-Thru ruler to draw a ¼″ seam line on each side of the diagonal line (Fig. 10-4). (Always use the same side of the ruler when drawing these lines, as there are variations.)

5. Pin each piece of light fabric right sides together with a piece of dark fabric. Do not place pins on seam lines.

6. Sew on the seam lines you marked in Step 4. Start at the corner top and work your way to one side (see arrows, Fig. 10-4). Then go back to the corner and work in the other direction. You do not want to sew to one edge, then turn around and sew back to the start. It can twist the fabric.

7. Sew this many light/dark pairs:

Crib	Twin	Full	Queen	King
2	4	4	6	8

8. Cut the triangles apart on the cutting lines (the solid lines in Fig. 10-4). Press the triangles toward the dark side (Fig. 10-5). Clip off the tips that stick out. The stitching in the triangle tips pulls right out. Set these triangles aside for now.

9. Sew the light and dark strips together that measure:

	Crib	Twin	Full	Queen	King
	1½″ × 56″	2½″ × 104″	2″ × 126″	2½″ × 112″	2½″ × 108″
				2½″ × 54″	

Do this the following number of times:

	Crib	Twin	Full	Queen	King
	4	4	4	4 + 6*	8

* For queen size there are four 2½″ × 112″ and six pieces 2½″ × 54″

Press these with seams toward the dark.

10. Take this many light/dark strips:

	Crib	Twin	Full	Queen	King
	2	2	2	4*	4

* 2½″ × 112″ only

Slice them every:

	Crib	Twin	Full	Queen	King
	2½″	4½″	3½″	4½″	4½″

These are your light/dark squares (Fig. 10-6).

Fig. 10-6

11. Take the remaining light/dark strips:

	Crib	Twin	Full	Queen	King
	2	2	2	6*	4

* 2½″ × 54″

Take strips of light fabric for centers as follows:

	Crib	Twin	Full	Queen	King
Number of slices	1	1	1	3	2
Size of slices	2½″ × 56″	4½″ × 100″	3½″ × 126″	4½″ × 54″	4½″ × 108″

Fig. 10-7

Sew it between two light/dark strips in the configuration shown in Fig. 10-7. Number of unts to sew:

	Crib	Twin	Full	Queen	King
	1	1	1	3	2

12. Slice these into slices this wide:

	Crib	Twin	Full	Queen	King
	2½″	4½″	3½″	4½″	4½″

You will need the following number of slices:

	Crib	Twin	Full	Queen	King
	22	22	36	36	45

This is your middle row of the Churn Dash.

13. Let's form the top and bottom of the pattern. Take your half-square triangle units and stack them next to the machine. Lay one on the machine right side up, dark corner in the lower right corner. Lay a light/dark square from Step 10 right side down, dark at the bottom. Sew these together (Fig. 10-8), feeding them into the machine and not clipping the threads until you have sewn:

Fig. 10-8

	Crib	Twin	Full	Queen	King
	44	44	72	72	90

Press away from the triangles.

14. Sew another triangle unit onto the other end as shown in Fig. 10-9.

Fig. 10-9

15. You can now piece all three rows (Fig. 10-10). Sew Row 1 to Row 2. Make sure Row 2 is on top as you sew. It will help you to lock in your seams. Press toward Row 2. Sew on Row 3 with Row 2 on top. Press toward Row 2. Your pieced blocks are complete (Fig. 10-11). At this point you need your plain squares. The Quilter's Rule 12½″ square works great for all sizes. Cut a strip and then slice your blocks from it. Stack your plain blocks up, paying attention to the direction of the grain. You will be sewing on the lengthwise grain.

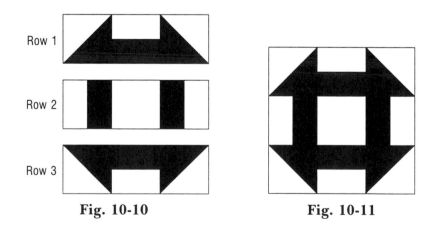

Row 1

Row 2

Row 3

Fig. 10-10

Fig. 10-11

16. Sew the following number of pairs of pieced blocks and plain blocks:

	Crib	Twin	Full	Queen	King
	14	14	27	27	36

17. Sew the pairs together to form the following number of rows:

Crib	Twin	Full	Queen	King
7	7	9	9	9

Each row should have the following number of pairs (blocks):

Crib	Twin	Full	Queen	King
2 pairs	2 pairs	3 pairs	3 pairs	4 pairs
(4 blocks)	(4 blocks)	(6 blocks)	(6 blocks)	(8 blocks)

18. Arrange all rows to begin with the pieced block. To the *end* of each *odd* row, add one pieced block. To the *beginning* of each *even* row, add one plain block. If you are making a crib-size quilt, you will have four Churn Dash blocks left over for the border. For all other sizes, make four 6″ Churn Dash blocks for your border.

19. Press the seams toward the plain block. Now sew your rows together.

20. This quilt will have a pieced border. Sew a light border strip between two dark border strips (Fig. 10-12). Do this four times. Press the seams toward the dark. Measure the length and width of the quilt top. Cut two of the border units the length and two the width. Sew the two length borders to the length of your quilt top (Fig. 10-13). Sew a Churn Dash block to each end of your top and bottom border strips (Fig. 10-14). Sew on these borders. One to the top, one to the bottom as shown in Fig. 10-1.

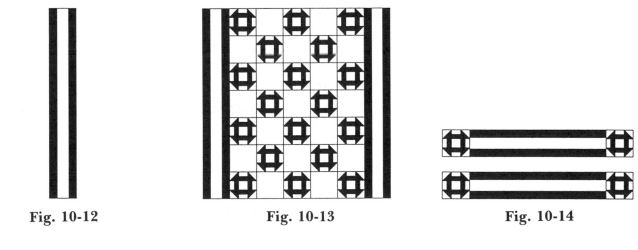

Fig. 10-12   Fig. 10-13   Fig. 10-14

Finishing

After you baste, you are ready to quilt! See Chapter 1 for information on basting, quilting, and tying.

Chapter 11

Sailboat

My Sailboat (Fig. 11-1) quilt started as a late-night need for a quick baby quilt. I started during prime time with my fabric washed and ironed. At 10:00 P.M. my sails were finished and I set them up with the background. By 11:30, my sails and boats were connected. "The Tonight Show" saw the blocks assembled and sashed. I decided against "Late Night" so I attached the borders the next day. I give only the crib and twin sizes here because I see this as a child's quilt. Enjoy!

Fig. 11-1

Slicing

Slice your fabric according to the following charts.

Dimensions of Quilts, Sailboat

	Crib	Twin
Finished size	40″ × 55″	64″ × 95″
Size of blocks	12″	12″
Number of blocks	6	15
Number of blocks across	2	3
Number of blocks down	3	5
Sashing	2½″	3½″
Borders (finished size)	1½″, 3″	2½″, 4½″

Fabric Requirements, Sailboat

	Crib	Twin
Sails (Fabric 1)	½ yd	1 yd
Background (Fabric 2)	1½ yds	2½ yds
Boats and inner border, binding (Fabric 3)	1½ yds	3 yds
Water and outside border (Fabric 4)	1½ yds	3 yds

Grid Requirements for Half-Square Triangles, Sailboat

	Crib	Twin
Grid size	12″ × 16″ 3 sq. × 4 sq.	12″ × 16″ 3 sq. × 4 sq.
Number of grid sheets	1	3
Size of squares	3⅞″	3⅞″
Number of half-square triangle units needed	24	60

Slicing Information, Sailboat

Note: Before you begin slicing, you will need to draw a cutting diagram for each fabric. See Chapter 1, page 4.

	Crib	Twin
Fabric 1		
Sails	1 grid sheet 12″ × 16″	3 grid sheets 12″ × 16″
Fabric 2		
Background	1 grid sheet 12″ × 16″	3 grid sheets 12″ × 16″
Vertical sashing	3 pieces 3″ × 42″	4 pieces 4″ × 84″

	Crib	Twin
Top and bottom sashing	2 pieces 3″×32″	2 pieces 4″×50½″
Horizontal sashing between blocks	1 piece 3″×54″	2 pieces 4″×90″
Background	2 pieces 3½″×54″	2 pieces 3½″×90″
Under boat	6 squares 3⅞″ cut in half for triangles	15 squares 3⅞″ cut in half for triangles
Fabric 3		
Boats	2 pieces 3½″×54″	2 pieces 3½″×108″
Inner border	4 pieces 2″×54″	4 pieces 3″×108″
Binding	4 pieces 2″×54″	4 pieces 2″×108″
Fabric 4		
Water	2 pieces 3½″×54″	2 pieces 3½″×108″
Outside border	4 pieces 3½″×54″	4 pieces 5″×108″

Piecing

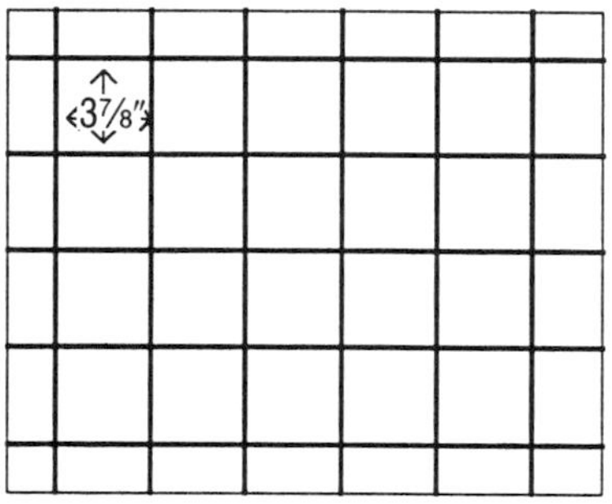

1. We will start by making half-square triangles on a grid sheet. Take a sheet of graph paper, 17″ × 22″ (8 squares to the inch). Carefully draw a grid on it, with the lines 3⅞″ apart (Fig. 11-2). You can fit 20 whole squares on one sheet of graph paper.

2. Lay a piece of light fabric (12″ × 16″) right side down on the paper. You may want to lightly tape your fabric in place.

3. Transfer the lines from the paper to the fabric. You will be able to fit 12 squares on the fabric. An easy way to do this is to use a long straightedge. Lay it on top of the fabric and line it up with the outside lines on your paper (Fig. 11-3).

Fig. 11-2

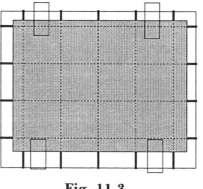

Fig. 11-3

4. With your Quilt-N-Sew or C-Thru ruler, draw a diagonal line through each square as shown in Fig. 11-4.

5. Draw a ¼″ seam line on each side of the diagonal line (Fig. 11-4). (Use the same side of the ruler when drawing these lines, as there are variations).

6. Pin light fabric right sides together to a piece of dark fabric. Do not place your pins on the seam lines.

7. Start sewing on the seam line in one corner of the grid (see arrows, Fig. 11-4). Then go back to the upper left-hand corner and sew on the next seam line. Sew one grid sheet for a crib-size quilt and three for a twin-size quilt. You need 12 squares for the crib size, 30 for the twin.

8. Cut the triangles apart on the cutting lines (the solid lines in Fig. 11-4).

9. Press the triangles toward the dark side (Fig. 11-5).

10. Trim off the little side tips. You need 24 half-square triangle units for a crib-size quilt and 60 triangles for a twin-size quilt.

11. Let's sew the sails together. Lay one half-square triangle unit right side up with the dark portion in the lower right-hand corner. Place another on top, right side down, dark in the lower left-hand corner. Sew all of your half-square triangle units into pairs (Fig. 11-6). Half of your pairs (six for a crib-size quilt and 15 for a twin-size quilt) will have top sails. Press the connecting seam toward the dark side. The other half will have bottom sails. Press the connecting seam of those toward the light side.

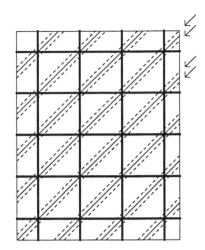

Fig. 11-4

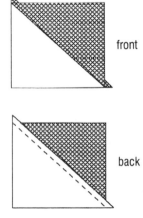

front

back

Fig. 11-5

Fig. 11-6

12. Now sew top sail pairs to bottom sail pairs to form the square shown in Fig. 11-7. The seam on top should be facing the sewing machine needle. Lock in your seams and hold the seam in place as you sew your ¼″ seam. Press your new seam down.

13. At this point it doesn't hurt to see if all your sails are blowing in the same direction (Fig. 11-7).

14. Next take a 3″ wide strip of background fabric and attach your sails to it. Lay the strip on the sewing machine right side up. Place your sails right side down. You will be sewing on the dark side first. Leave a scant ¼″ between sail squares.

15. After you have sewn them all on to the background strips, cut them apart (Fig. 11-8). Then sew the other side to another strip.

Fig. 11-7

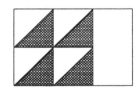

Fig. 11-8

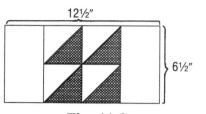

Fig. 11-9

You will be sewing on the light side now. Press both seams away from the sails. Your piece should now be 12½″ × 6½″ (Fig. 11-9).

16. Use a large ruler (6½″ × 24″) to square up this section. Lay the pieced rectangle on your cutting mat and place the ruler on top. Trim off any extra from the background strip. Turn your piece 180 degrees. Trim other side.

17. Now it's time to make the boat. Take your 3½″-wide strip of boat fabric and slice it into 12½″ pieces.

18. One at a time, fold each piece in half so that it is 3½″ × 6¼″. On one edge only, not the folded side, take off a 3¼″ triangle (Fig. 11-10). When you open your folded piece, you will have the boat shape (Fig. 11-11).

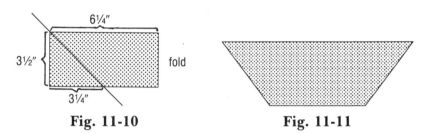

Fig. 11-10   **Fig. 11-11**

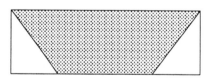

Fig. 11-12

19. Now take a piece of background fabric and cut six 3⅞″ squares for a crib-size quilt and fifteen 3⅞″ squares for a twin size quilt. Cut these in half on the diagonal to make 12 triangles for a crib-size quilt and 30 triangles for a twin-size quilt. Sew these triangles to the slanted edges of the boat shape (Fig. 11-12). Press the seam toward the light. (It wants to go there anyway.)

20. Sew the top of the boat to the bottom of the sails. Press this seam in the direction of the boat.

21. Take a 3½″ strip of water fabric and lay it right side up on the sewing machine. Lay your block right side down. You are sewing the water fabric to the bottom of the boat. Seam all blocks.

22. Cut these apart and square up your block again (Fig. 11-13). You are ready for the sashing.

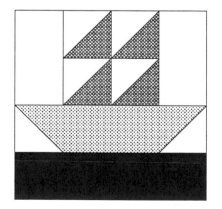

Fig. 11-13

23. Now sew a strip of sashing (background) fabric between the blocks as shown in Fig. 11-14. You will need three blocks down for the crib size, five for the twin size. Sew two columns for the crib-size quilt and three columns for the twin-size quilt.

24. Lay one column right side down on a vertical sash slice. You will be sewing from the bottom of that row, with the sailboats upside-down.

25. As you look at the row from the front, you have sewn on the right-hand side of the row. Sew a strip of sashing fabric on the left.

26. Sew your first column to your next column. The best way to match up the sailboats is to mark lightly on the wrong side of the sashing a line showing the block seam line. You can then pin this line to the block intersections in Column 2. Press toward the sashing.

27. If you are making the *crib quilt,* sew on your last vertical sashing (Fig. 11-15). For a *twin,* sew on another vertical sashing strip. Press. Sew on Column 3; then after pressing, sew on the last vertical sashing.

28. Square off the top and bottom edges.

29. Sew on the top and bottom sashing. Press and square all corners. Sew on the first border. Sew sides first, then top and bottom. The last border is the one you made the "water" out of. Press, square, and get ready to baste.

Finishing

Review Chapter 1 for your options on basting, tying, and quilting.

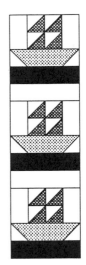

Fig. 11-14

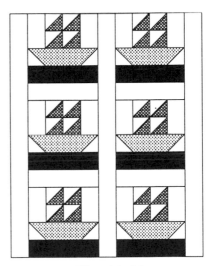

Fig. 11-15

ADVANCED
QUILTS BY THE SLICE

Chapter 12

Bear's Paw

The Bear's Paw is a fine example of an early American pioneer pattern (Fig. 12-1A). Many Bear's Paw quilts were made with a sawtooth border (Fig. 12-1B). Indigo blue and white or red and white were popular colors for the quilts. Setting it on the diagonal, with solid alternate blocks, adds to the traditional look.

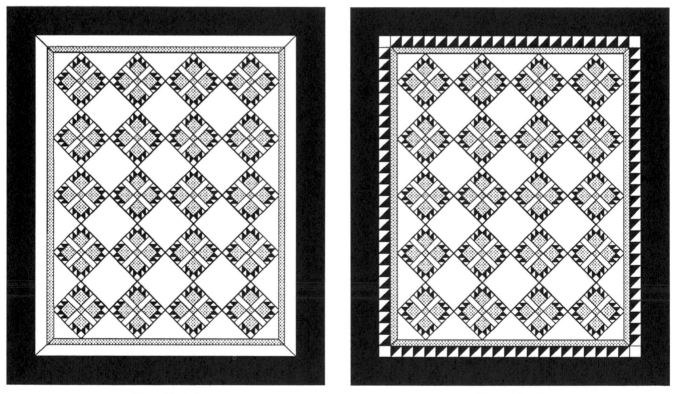

Fig. 12-1A   **Fig. 12-1B**

If you want a sawtooth border, you can make one quickly by using the same grid you used for the claws. See the chart Fabric and Grid Requirements for Sawtooth Border, Bear's Paw.

Slicing

Slice your fabric according to the following charts.

Dimensions of Quilts, Bear's Paw

	Crib	Twin	Full	Queen/King
Finished size	44″ × 54″	69½″ × 108¾″	92″ × 112″	112½″ × 112½″
Size of blocks	7″	14″	14″	14″
Total number of blocks	32	23	32	41
Number of blocks across	4	3	4	5
Number of blocks down	5	5	5	5
Number of pieced blocks	20	15	20	25
Number of solid blocks	12	8	12	16
Number of side triangles	16	14	16	18
Borders (finished width)	2″	2″, 3″	2½″, 4″	3″, 4″

Fabric Requirements, Bear's Paw

	Crib	Twin	Full	Queen/King
Claws (darkest)	1½ yds	3 yds	3½ yds	4 yds
Background (lightest)	1¾ yds	4¾ yds	5¼ yds	8 yds
Paws	½ yd	1¼ yds	1½ yds	2 yds

Slicing Information for Blocks, Bear's Paw

Note: Before slicing, you will need to draw a cutting diagram for each fabric. See Chapter 1, page 4.

	Crib	Twin	Full	Queen/King
Claws				
Number of slices	5	4	6	7
Size of slices	16″ × 8″	15″ × 18″	15″ × 18″	15″ × 18″
Background				
Number of slices	5	4	6	7
Size of slices	16″ × 8″	15″ × 18″	15″ × 18″	15″ × 18″
Number of slices	3	4	6	7
Size of slices	1½″ × 45″	2½″ × 108″	2½″ × 108″	2½″ 117″

	Crib	Twin	Full	Queen/King
Number of slices	1	1	1	1
Size of slices	3½″ × 45″	6½″ × 108″	6½″ × 108″	6½″ 117″
Number of slices	12	8	12	16
Size of slices	7½″ × 7½″	14½″ × 14½″	14½″ × 14½″	14½″ × 14½″
Number of slices	8	7	8	9
Size of slices	8″ × 8″ (cut on diagonal to form 16 triangles)	15″ × 15″ (cut on diagonal to form 14 triangles)	15″ × 15″ (cut on diagonal to form 16 triangles)	15″ × 15″ (cut on diagonal to form 18 triangles)
Paws				
Number of slices	10	6	5	7
Size of slices	2½″ × 18″	4½″ × 45″	4½″ × 54″	4½″ × 72″
Number of slices (center row)	2	2	2	4
Size of slices	1½″ × 18″	2½″ × 45″	2½″ × 54″	2½″ × 72″

Grid Requirements for Half-Square Triangles, Bear's Paw

	Crib	Twin	Full	Queen/King
Grid size	16″ × 8″ 8 sq. × 4 sq.	15″ × 18″ 5 sq. × 6 sq.	15″ × 18″ 5 sq. × 6 sq.	15″ × 18″ 5 sq. × 6 sq.
Number of grid sheets	5	4	6	7
Size of squares	1⅞″	2⅞″	2⅞″	2⅞″
Number of half-square triangle units needed	320	240	320	400

Slicing Information for Borders and Binding, Bear's Paw

	Crib	Twin	Full	Queen/King
Outside borders (claws fabric)				
Number of slices	4	4	4	4
Size of slices	2½″ × 54″	3½″ × 108″	4½″ × 108″	4½″ × 117″
Binding (claws fabric)				
Number of slices	4	4	4	4
Size of slices	2″ × 54″	2″ × 108″	2″ × 108″	2″ × 117″
Inner border (background fabric)				
Number of slices	—	4	4	4
Size of slices	—	2½″ × 108″	3″ × 108″	3½″ × 117″

Fabric and Grid Requirements for Sawtooth Border, Bear's Paw

	Crib	Twin	Full	Queen/King
Dark (claws)	¼ yd	1¼ yds	1½ yds	2 yds
Light (background)	¼ yd	1¼ yds	1½ yds	2 yds
Number of triangle pairs	160	300	332	370
Grid sheet size	16″×8″	15″×18″	15″×18″	15″×18″
Number of grid sheets	2	5	6	7

Piecing

We will start by making the claws. These half-square triangles will be made with the same type of grid used in the Churn Dash (Chapter 10). Our first job is quick piecing the triangles for the claws. It is odd to say "quick piecing" in the same context as Bear's Paw. It will take a lot of time to make this quilt. These are the most accurate, "quick" methods I know to finish the task. Don't be so discouraged that you decide not to start this quilt. Just be aware of what is facing you—and enjoy.

1. Take a sheet of graph paper, 17″ × 22″ (8 squares to the inch). Carefully draw a grid on it, with the lines at intervals as follows:

Crib	Twin	Full	Queen/King
1⅞″	2⅞″	2⅞″	2⅞″

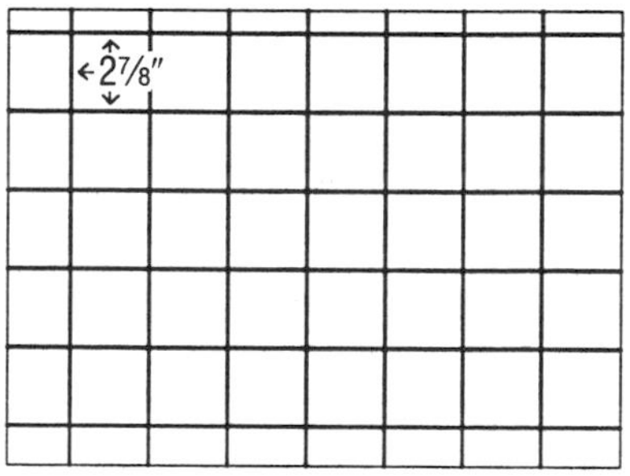

Extend your lines to the edges of the graph paper. Fig. 12-2 shows the grid for twin, full, or queen/king. Draw the following number of whole squares on your sheet of graph paper:

Crib	Twin	Full	Queen/King
32	30	30	30

Note: You will not fill the graph paper sheet for the crib size. You will be more accurate drawing just 32 whole squares.

2. Lay a piece of light fabric on the paper right side down. (Check size under "Claws" in the chart Slicing Information for Blocks, Bear's Paw. You may want to tape your fabric in place. Transfer the lines from the paper to the fabric (Fig. 12-3). An easy way to do this is to use a long straightedge. Lay it on top of the fabric and line it up with the outside lines on your paper. For this part I use a very sharp #2 pencil. Mark dark enough to see, but do not make a big black line. I never use a regular lead pencil on the right side of a quilt.

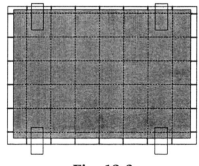

Fig. 12-2

Fig. 12-3

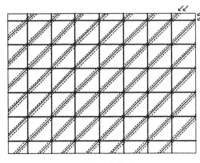

Fig. 12-4

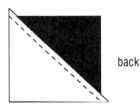

front

back

Fig. 12-5

3. After you have transferred the lines, draw a diagonal line with your Quilt-N-Sew ruler through each square. Eventually, these will be your cutting lines. Now draw a ¼″ seam line on each side of the diagonal line (Fig. 12-4). (Always use the same side of the ruler when drawing these lines, as there are variations.)

4. Pin light fabric right sides together to a piece of dark fabric the same size. Do not place your pins on the seam lines. It is important that your sewing machine be adjusted correctly. If the tension is too tight, the seams will pucker.

5. Start sewing on the seam line in an upper corner of the grid. Then go back to the corner and sew on the next seam line to the right. Sew every seam line until you finish the right side of the grid. After sewing that half, go back to the upper corner and sew the seam to the left of the corner. Then sew every seam line until the entire grid is sewn. You will be sewing over the tips of the adjacent triangles. That is all right. You do not want to sew the lines from different directions. This could pull your fabric and cause it to twist. Sew the following number of light/dark pairs:

Crib	Twin	Full	Queen/King
5	4	6	7

6. Cut the triangles apart on the diagonal, horizontal, and vertical cutting lines (the solid lines in Fig. 12-4). Press the triangles toward the dark side (Fig. 12-5). Trim off the little side tips. You should now have this many half-square triangle units:

Crib	Twin	Full	Queen/King
320	240	320	400

7. Let's put the claws together. Take two half-square triangle units. Stitch them together with a ¼″ seam to form the unit shown in Fig. 12-6. Press toward dark. Do this the following number of times:

Crib	Twin	Full	Queen/King
80	60	80	100

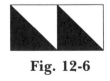

Fig. 12-6

You are using only half of your triangle squares for this step. Save the rest for later.

8. To sew this unit to a background strip, take a strip of background fabric this wide:

	Crib	Twin	Full	Queen/King
	1½″	2½″	2½″	2½″

Lay it right side up on the sewing machine. Place your triangle strip (two triangle squares sewn together) as shown in Fig. 12-7, leaving a scant ¼″ between each triangle strip. This will help with squaring later. Seam. You will need to sew the following number of triangle strips:

	Crib	Twin	Full	Queen/King
	80	60	80	100

9. Cut these apart. Press the seam to the plain square. (That is the direction it will want to go to anyway.)

10. Lay these units on your cutting mat one at a time to square them up. Place your Quilter's Rule over the piece lengthwise. The triangle strip should be 2½″ wide (1½″ for crib). Everything else can be trimmed off. Turn the strip around 180 degrees and trim off the other side. Set aside. You will use four of these units in each block.

11. Take your remaining triangle squares. Sew with ¼″ seam into pairs as shown in Fig. 12-8. Press toward dark.

12. Now take a strip of paw fabric. The width will measure:

	Crib	Twin	Full	Queen/King
	2½″	4½″	4½″	4½″

Lay it right side up on the machine. Lay the triangle strips you made in Step 11 on top, right side down, both darks in lower right corner. Leave a scant ¼″ between units for squaring up later. Fill up your paw strips with units. Seam. Do this the following number of times:

	Crib	Twin	Full	Queen/King
	80	60	80	100

13. Cut them apart. The finished width should be 4½″ except for the crib, which will be 2½″. Press toward large block.

14. Lay your ruler on top of the paw strip and trim it to the finished width. You will be able to see right away where it might need to be trimmed.

15. Sew this unit to the first unit that you made in Steps 8 through 10 (Fig. 12-9). This completes one paw. You will need four per block.

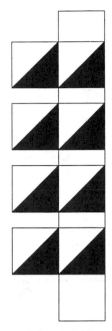

Fig. 12-7

Fig. 12-8

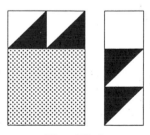

Fig. 12-9

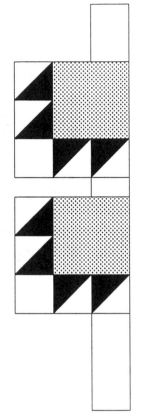

Fig. 12-10

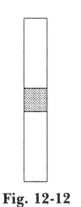

Fig. 12-12

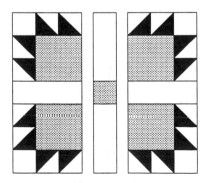

Fig. 12-13

16. Sew half of these paws to a strip of background this wide:

	Crib	Twin	Full	Queen/King
	1½″	2½″	2½″	2½″

Lay the background strip on the machine right side up. Lay the paw right side down, with the paw square in upper right-hand corner (Fig. 12-10). Here again, leave a scant ¼″ space between blocks. This will given you room to square it up. Sew with a ¼″ seam.

17. Cut the paws apart and press the seam toward the background strip.

18. Square the paws. Then sew another paw to the other side of the background strip. Make sure the claws point in opposite directions (Fig. 12-11). You will need two of these units for each block.

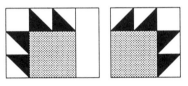

Fig. 12-11

19. You have just completed the top and bottom of the block; all you need is the center row. Make this by sewing your narrower strips of paws fabric between two strips of background fabric. The background fabric strips will be this wide:

	Crib	Twin	Full	Queen/King
	3½″	6½″	6½″	6½″

Cut them to the same length as your narrower paws strips before you sew. After sewing, slice this into the following widths (Fig. 12-12):

	Crib	Twin	Full	Queen/King
	1½″	2½″	2½″	2½″

20. Sew your blocks together (Fig. 12-13).

21. We will be setting this quilt on point. The rows will be sewn diagonally. You will need the following number of setting triangles for the sides:

	Crib	Twin	Full	Queen/King
	16	14	16	18

Cut these as squares, then cut them diagonally into triangles. (Cut one of the squares into four triangles for the corners.) Before cutting the triangles, machine baste a scant ¼″ on each side of the diagonal. This will help keep your bias lines from stretching (Fig 12-14). Trim the squares you sliced earlier (see Slicing Information for Blocks, Bear's Paw, pages 101–102) as follows:

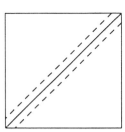

Fig. 12-14

	Crib	Twin	Full	Queen/King
Number of squares	8	7	8	9
Size	7⅞″	14⅞″	14⅞″	14⅞″

Lay out the blocks in rows running diagonally. Use Fig. 12-1A or B as a guide. Sew the side triangles on as shown. I sew on the four corner triangles last. Press the seams toward the plain blocks. Sew the rows together locking in the seam intersections. Sew on the corners. They will be too big. Trim them after they are sewn on.

Borders

If you are using the sawtooth border, start with a narrow border of background fabric, the sawtooth, and then finish with a wider border of background. If you are not using the sawtooth, start with a narrow border of the medium (paws), a wider border of background and finish with a wide border of dark (claws).

Finishing

Review your options for basting, tying, and quilting in Chapter 1.

Chapter 13

Lone Star

Lone Star quilts have been around for over 150 years (Figs. 13-1A, 13-1B). They have been called many things: Texas Star, Star of Bethlehem, Star of the East, Virginia Star, Radiant Star—and difficult. I would like to change the last description from "difficult" to "challenging." With good technique and patience, you can make one today (or maybe tomorrow).

Fig. 13-1A

Fig. 13-1B

The perfect ruler has been designed to make this quilt easier—the Acu Angle by Jackie Black of Canada. Virginia Gossling of Toronto, Canada, brought these rulers to my attention at her quilt shop, "Quilting Bee." I'm very grateful for the sharing. Check your local quilt supply store for them. They come in 1″, 2″, and 2½″ (finished measurement of the ruler along the side). You can also use the 45° angle of your large ruler to cut these slices, but be careful. That is such a critical step that you must be absolutely accurate.

I find that when I use the Acu Angle ruler, I need to change the seam allowance slightly on my sewing machine. The ruler's ¼″ is a little different from that on my C-Thru ruler.

It is possible to alter the size of your star in two ways: change the size of the diamond or change the number of diamonds in a point of your star.

This quilt in crib size is a project that is less expensive if you cut your fabric on the crosswise grain (width); however, it is certainly easier on the lengthwise grain. You will always have two bias sides to your diamond, so it is nice not to have the other two sides stretchy also, as they are if cut on the crosswise grain. Use closely woven cotton. A Lone Star is not a project for slipping in a little polyester blend.

In these instructions, I have included eight options for the star: you can make it with three, four, six, or seven rows of diamonds. The diamonds can be 2″ or 2½″. I also include instructions for two great pieced borders.

If you choose three rows of 2″ diamonds, your star would measure 27″ square. With borders it would be a great wall hanging or crib quilt. It's a good place to begin. The directions here are for a four-row star. Learn the technique before you make a larger size. If you choose three rows of 2½″ diamonds, your star will be 37″ square. For a bed-size quilt, you want the star to cover the top of the bed; the borders hang down the sides. The 37″ star would cover the width of a twin bed. It is difficult to elongate this star to turn it into a twin-size quilt. (A twin-size bed measures 37″ × 75″.) The 6-row 2″ or 7-row 2½″ sizes given in the following charts will make a queen-size quilt. The 7-row 2″ size will make a full-size quilt, and the 6-row 2½″ size will make a king-size quilt.

Once you have chosen your diamond size and number of rows, think about how you want to shade it. The easiest to plan is the Reverse-Repeat in which your center diamond and the outside diamond are the same (Fig. 13-1 A or B).

In the Radiant Star pattern, frequently seen in old Amish quilts, the center is very light, with each row getting darker out to the points, or just the opposite, with the center dark and each row getting lighter.

Of course, there are many other ways to lay out your star. Draw a large diamond and divide it into small diamonds—experiment. Keep in mind that you want your outer points to show up on your background fabric.

Slicing

You will need one strip 42″ long for each 2″ or 2½″ diamond in your point. Thus for a three-row design, you need the following for the entire star: 2 slices of A fabric, 4 slices of B fabric, and 3 slices of C fabric. If you are using the 2″ diamond, add ½″ for your ¼″ seam allowances. That means:

> 2 slices of A fabric (2½″ × 42″ = 5″ × 42″ = ¼ yd)
> 4 slices of B fabric (2½″ × 42″ = 10″ × 42″ = ½ yd)
> 3 slices of C fabric (2½″ × 42″ = 7½″ × 42″ = ⅓ yd)

This does not allow for border, just the star. I've allowed a little extra fabric so you can straighten the crosswise grain. Now add borders, binding, and background. With this background information you can plan your own quilt. Or you can use the following charts to choose the best size for you. Feel free to change borders and rearrange fabrics. Or omit some of the borders to make a smaller quilt. I always use the background fabric as the inner border. Let's be realistic: If your points are not precise, this way they will float and no one will notice.

Lone Star, 2″ Diamond, 3 Rows

Finished size of quilt	36″ × 36″
Borders, finished size	1½″, 3″
Fabric requirements	
A (includes outer border and binding)	1 yd
B	½ yd
C	⅓ yd
Background and inner border	1 yd
Slices needed	
A	2 slices, 2½″ × 42″
B	4 slices, 2½″ × 42″
C	3 slices, 2½″ × 42″
Inner border (background)	4 slices, 2″ × 42″
Outer border (A)	4 slices, 3½″ × 42″
Binding (A)	4 slices, 2″ × 42″

Lone Star, 2″ Diamond, 4 Rows

Finished size of quilt	48″ × 48″
Borders, finished size	2″, 3½″
Fabric requirements	
A (includes outer border and binding)	1¼ yds (cut on length)
B	½ yd
C	⅝ yd
D	½ yd
Background and inner border	1¼ yds
Slices needed	
A	2 slices, 2½″ × 45″ (on length)
B	4 slices, 2½″ × 42″
C	6 slices, 2½″ × 42″
D	4 slices, 2½″ × 42″
Inner border (background)	4 slices, 2″ × 42″
Outer border (A)	4 slices, 4″ × 45″
Binding (A)	5 slices, 2″ × 45″

Lone Star, 2″ Diamond, 6 Rows

Finished size of quilt	92″ × 92″ (queen)
Borders, finished size	1½″, 2½″, 4″*, 5½″
Fabric requirements	
A (includes pieced border)	1½ yds (cut on length)
B	½ yd
C	⅝ yd
D	¾ yd
E (includes binding)	1½ yds (cut on length)
F (includes pieced border and borders 2 and 4)	5 yds (cut on length)
Background and inner border	3 yds
Slices needed	
A	2 slices, 2½″ × 42″ (on length)
B	4 slices, 2½″ × 42″
C	6 slices, 2½″ × 42″
D	8 slices, 2½″ × 42″
E	10 slices, 2½″ × 42″
F	6 slices, 2½″ × 42″
Inner border (background)	4 slices, 2″ × 72″
Second border F	4 slices, 3″ × 75″
Pieced border A	10 slices, 2½″ × 54″
Pieced border F	5 slices, 2½″ × 54″
Outer border F	4 slices, 6″ × 108″
Binding F	7 slices, 2″ × 54″

*The 4″ border is a Seminole pieced border. Fabric is included.

Lone Star, 2″ Diamond, 7 Rows

Finished size of quilt	89″ × 89″ (full)
Borders, finished size	1½″, 2½″, 5½″
Fabric requirements	
A (includes outer border)	3 yds (cut on length)
B	½ yd
C	⅝ yd
D	¾ yd
E	3 yds (cut on length)
F	1¼ yds (cut on length)
G	¾ yd
Background and inner border	3 yds

Lone Star, 2″ Diamond, 7 Rows (*continued*)

Slices needed	
A	2 slices, 2½″ × 42″ (cut on length)
B	4 slices, 2½″ × 42″
C	6 slices, 2½″ × 42″
D	8 slices, 2½″ × 42″
E	10 slices, 2½″ × 42″ (cut on length)
F	12 slices, 2½″ × 42″ (cut on length)
G	7 slices, 2½″ × 42″
Inner border	4 slices, 2″ × 75″
Middle border E	4 slices, 3″ × 90″
Outer border A	4 slices, 6″ × 90″
Binding A	4 slices, 2″ × 108″

Lone Star, 2½″ Diamond, 3 Rows

Finished size of quilt	42″ × 42″
Borders, finished size	1″, 1½″
Fabric requirements	
A (includes outer border and binding)	1¼ yds (cut on length)
B	½ yd
C	⅓ yd
Background and inner border	1¼ yds (cut on length)
Slices needed	
A	2 slices, 3″ × 45″
B	4 slices, 3″ × 42″
C	3 slices, 3″ × 42″
Inner border (background)	4 slices, 1½″ × 45″
Outer border (A)	4 slices, 2″ × 45″
Binding (A)	4 slices, 2″ × 45″

Lone Star, 2½″ Diamond, 4 Rows

Finished size of quilt	59″ × 59″
Borders, finished size	1½″, 3½″
Fabric requirements	
A (includes outer border and binding)	1¾ yds (cut on length)
B	½ yd
C	¾ yd
D	½ yd
Background and inner border	1½ yds (cut on length)

Lone Star, 2½″ Diamond, 4 Rows (*continued*)

Slices needed

A	2 slices, 3″ × 42″ (cut on length)
B	4 slices, 3″ × 42″
C	6 slices, 3″ × 42″
D	4 slices, 3″ × 42″
Inner border (background)	4 slices, 2″ × 54″
Outer border (A)	4 slices, 4″ × 63″
Binding (A)	4 slices, 2″ × 63″

Lone Star, 2½″ Diamond, 6 Rows

Finished size of quilt	105″ × 105″ (king)
Borders, finished size	1½″, 2½″, 4″*, 2½″, 5″
Fabric requirements	
A (includes outer border)	3 yds
B	½ yd
C	¾ yd
D	1¼ yds
E	1¼ yds
F (includes pieced border)	3 yds
Background and inner border	4 yds
Slices needed	
A	2 slices, 3″ × 42″ (cut on length)
B	4 slices, 3″ × 42″
C	6 slices, 3″ × 42″
D	8 slices, 3″ × 42″ (cut on length)
E	10 slices, 3″ × 42″ (cut on length)
F	6 slices, 3″ × 42″ (cut on length)
Inner border	4 slices, 2″ × 72″
Second border (F)	4 slices, 3″ × 80″
Pieced border (A)	10 slices, 2½″ × 42″
Pieced border (F)	5 slices, 2½″ × 42″
Fourth border (F)	4 slices, 3″ × 95″
Final border (A)	4 slices, 5½″ × 108″
Binding (A)	4 slices, 2″ × 108″

*The 4″ border is a Seminole pieced border. Fabric is included.

Lone Star, 2½″ Diamond, 7 Rows

Finished size of quilt	96″ × 101″ (queen)
Borders, finished size	1½″, 2½″, 3½″
Pieced border, top and bottom	2″
Fabric requirements	
A (includes outer border and binding)	3 yds (cut on length)
B	¾ yd
C (includes middle border)	3 yds (cut on length)
D	1 yd
E	1 yd
F	1¼ yds (cut on length)
G	¾ yd
Background (includes inner border	4½ yds
Slices needed	
A	2 slices, 3″ × 42″ (cut on length)
B	4 slices, 3″ × 42″
C	6 slices, 3″ × 42″ (cut on length)
D	8 slices, 3″ × 42″
E	10 slices, 3″ × 42″
F	12 slices, 3″ × 42″
G	7 slices, 3″ × 42″
Inner border (background fabric)	4 slices, 2″ × 100″
Outer border (A)	4 slices, 4″ × 108″
Middle border (C)	4 slices, 3″ × 108″
Pieced border, top and bottom (A thru G)	2 slices of each fabric, 2½″ × 42″
Binding (A)	4 slices, 2″ × 108″

* The 2″ border is strip-pieced just like the row of the star.

Piecing

Now let's get down to business.

1. Piecing this quilt will not be as complicated as choosing the size you are going to do. Start by taking one strip of fabric 42″ long each time it is called for on your diamond drawing. Let's say you are making a Lone Star with 2″ diamonds and four rows. Check the charts to see how many slices you need of each fabric. After slicing your fabric, stack it in front of your machine in rows.

2. Now all you have to do is sew rows. Double-check your seam gauge. Make sure it matches the seam allowance on the ruler you will be using. Start Row 1 by laying Fabric A right side up on the sewing machine. Place Fabric B right side down. Fabric B needs to be staggered down 2½″ (Fig. 13-2). Sew a ¼″ seam down the length of the strip. Press the seam toward A.

3. Place this unit on the machine right side up. Place piece C right side down on top of piece B. Drop it down 2½″. Sew a ¼″ seam (Fig. 13-3). Press it toward B. Now add Fabric D in the same way (Fig. 13-4).

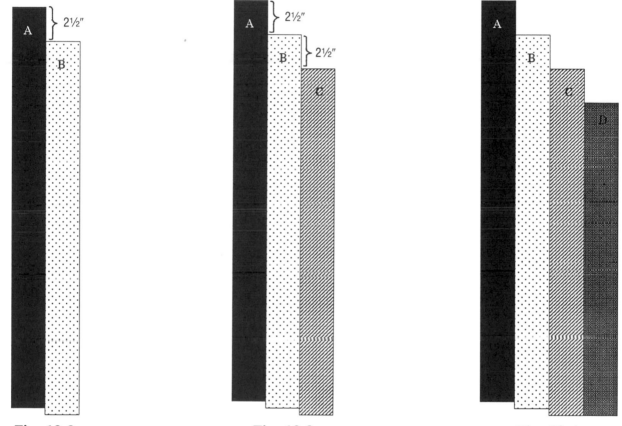

Fig. 13-2   Fig. 13-3   Fig. 13-4

4. Now make three more of these units, but with the fabrics in different order: BCDC, CDCB, and DCBA (Fig. 13-5).

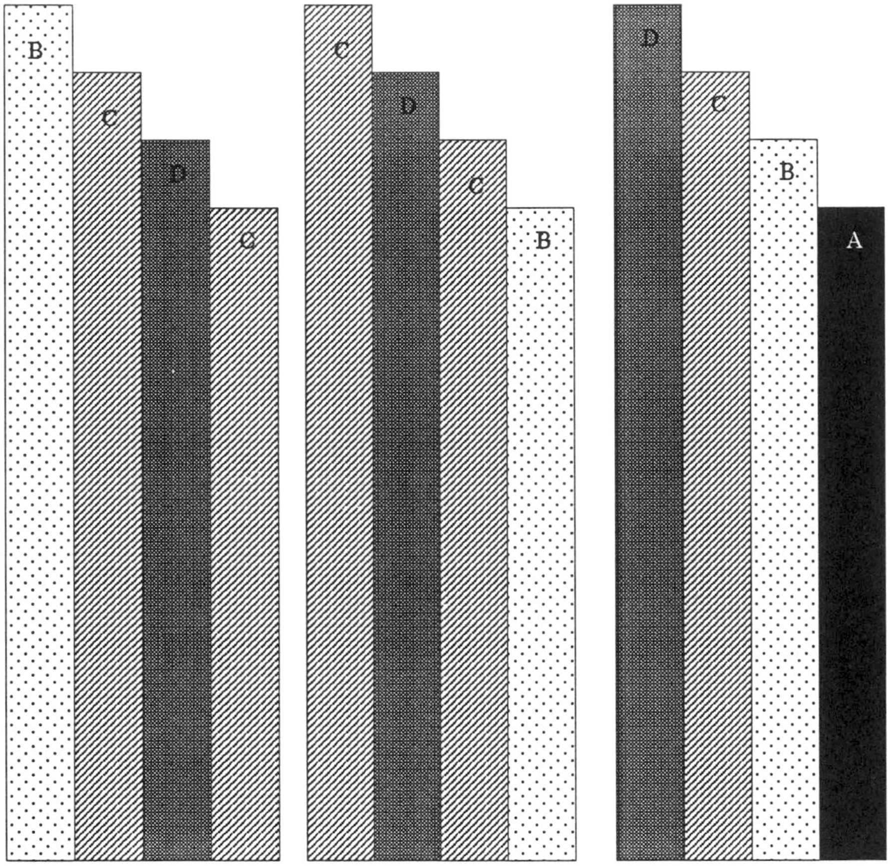

Fig. 13-5

Fig. 13-6

5. Slice eight pieces from each unit with your rotary cutter and Acu Angle ruler. Your seam lines should match the ruler seam lines (Fig. 13-6). If they do not, find out why. Are your seams pressed correctly? Are your seam allowances ¼″? Did you slice the right size strip? If you are not using an Acu-Angle, line up the 45° angle line of your large Quilter's Rule with the top slice of fabric for each unit. Slice along the edge of the ruler. Make sure you slice all strips starting at the same end of the fabric. That becomes more important if you are making more than three rows. On your four-row star, the rows are not interchangeable: they would be ABCD, BCDC, CDCB, DCBA. For a three-row star, though, you could reverse rows one and two (the three rows are ABC, BCB, and CBA). Now arrange your slices in rows, as shown in Fig. 13-7.

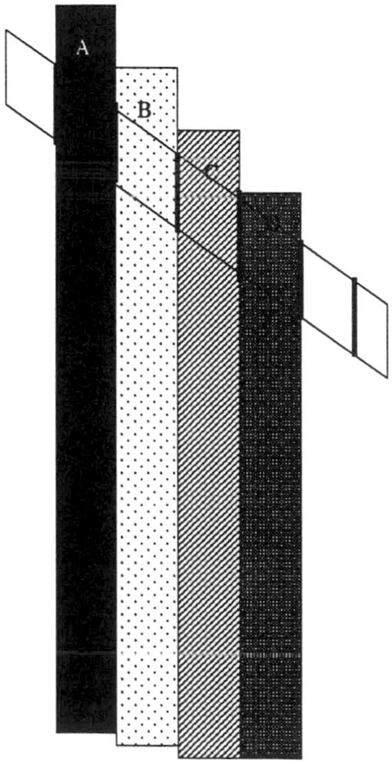

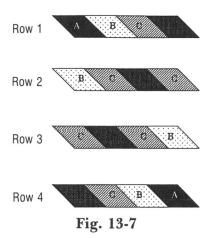

Row 1
Row 2
Row 3
Row 4

Fig. 13-7

6. With a lengthened stitch or with your machine set on basting, sew your rows together to form your first diamond (Fig. 13-8). This is just to see how the diamonds meet. You will restitch on a normal setting, if all is well. If not, it sure is easier to take out basting than regular stitching. If you have a needle down setting on your machine, this is a good time to use it. It will help keep the intersections of the seam allowances from slipping. I take my long needle and stick it in to the top strip (Row 2) B at the seam line ¼″ away from the edge. I stick it through to the bottom strip (Row 3) C right at the seam line. After "stabbing" the intersection you might feel more comfortable putting in a straight pin next to the long needle. Do this for all intersections. Sew this seam. If it is all right, sew it again on normal stitch length. Now sew seven more diamonds.

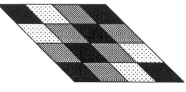

Fig. 13-8

7. Sew your eight diamonds into pairs (Fig. 13-9). Then sew two pairs into halves. Press your halves at this time. Press the seams joining the quarters so they will go in opposite directions when you sew your halves together. Before sewing these halves together, con-

Fig. 13-9

nect only 1″ in the center. Check to see if it looks good. If it does (let's hope so), sew from the center to the right, then from the center toward the left. Perfect (Fig. 13-10).

Fig. 13-10

8. Now measure for the background squares. I will give you the cut dimensions, but measure to see if yours match mine. The square must match your star. Don't forget to add seam allowances before you cut. You will also cut two squares for your four triangles. It is important to keep the straight of grain edges of your triangle against your stretchy star points, with the bias edge of the triangle on the outside edge of the quilt. Before you cut your square into triangles, staystitch on both sides of the center cutting line to prevent stretching. Here are my instructions for cutting your squares and triangles.

	2″ Diamond	2½″ Diamond
3 rows		
Cut 4 squares	9½″	11½″
Cut 2 squares for triangles	10″	12″
4 rows		
Cut 4 squares	12½″	15″
Cut 2 squares for triangles	13″	15½″

	2″ Diamond	**2½″ Diamond**
6 rows		
Cut 4 squares	18½″	22″
Cut 2 squares for triangles	19″	22½″
7 rows		
Cut 4 squares	21½″	25¾″
Cut 2 squares for triangles	22″	26¼″

9. I like to sew the background squares and triangles from the inside toward the star point. With the background piece on the bottom and the star on top, put the sewing machine needle into the intersection. Sew toward the star tip. Stop at the ¼″ intersection. Go back to the inside of the square or triangle; the star is now on the bottom. Sew from the inside to the star tip, again stopping ¼″ from the intersection. Do this for all of the background pieces.

10. The first border will be from the background fabric. Sew on sides first, then top and bottom. This is the Log Cabin Border method (see page 9).

11. After the inner border, you can go to the next border or piece a border to elongate your quilt. One simple pieced border (Fig. 13-1A) is made the same way you made your star slice. (I have allowed for this type of border in the chart for the 2½″ diamond with seven rows.) Cut two 2½″ × 42″ strips of each fabric. Sew them together as though you were making another star, with fabrics in ABCD order. Remember to drop down 2½″ as you stagger the strips. Slice as you did before (Fig. 13-6). Sew these slices together side to side. Make two rows of 37 diamonds each. Sew one to the top of the background border, one to the bottom.

Another pieced border is shown in Fig. 13-1B. I have allowed for this type of border in the charts for the six-row diamonds. This is a little more detailed. Cut ten strips of Fabric A, 2½″ × 42″. Cut five strips of Fabric F, 2½″ × 42″. Make five strip units of AFA. Use a medium and a dark; I allowed for Fabrics A and F in the 6-row charts. Do not stagger the ends. Press toward the dark. Slice into pieces 2½″ wide. Stagger these as you sew them together. You need about 18 slices per border piece. Press. From the back side draw a line ¼″ above the intersection at the top and bottom of the dark square. I usually sew a basting stitch inside this line before trimming.

Whenever I use this type of pieced border, I also use a "plug" border. It is rare that your pieced border will automatically fit your quilt top. It is easier to change the quilt than it is to change the border. The plug gives me the extra size I might need. I make the plug border strip a little longer than needed. For example, if my border measures 76″ (in 4″ increments) and my quilt measures 74″, I will "plug" up the difference with a 1″ border on each end. I measure carefully and cut the plug border to take up any slack in the top. I use lots of pins to make sure my pieced border does not stretch. This pieced border can be altered by trimming only the inner edge of the border strip and leaving the bottom as the edge of the quilt, otherwise I put on at least one more border.

Finishing

Review Chapter 1 for your options on basting, tying, and quilting.

Chapter 14

Mormor's Quilt

The Mormor's Quilt (Fig. 14-1) was brought to my attention by Lorene Gruber. She had made the quilt through a class at Quilter's Corner in Gainesville, Florida, given by Shirley Wengler. The quilt was so beautiful. The name *Mormor* is Scandinavian, meaning "grandmother." More specifically, it means "mother's mother."

Fig. 14-1

Two years after I saw Lorene's quilt, two ladies came in to my shop and asked me to help them make their Mormor's Quilt. They had purchased their fabric two years earlier after seeing Lorene's quilt in my shop. Lorene was back in Florida for the summer, so she couldn't help. What was I to do?

My first thought was to talk the ladies out of their beautiful discontinued Hoffman fabric. My second was to take a drawing of Lorene's quilt and make it happen for these ladies. Here is what I came up with. Their large floral Hoffman fabric became the background.

The main piece of the block is an elongated hexagon. You start with a rectangle and use a triangle pattern you'll make to trim off the corners. Strips of light, medium, and dark are sewn to the hexagon. A square is formed by adding triangles to two of the corners. Four of these squares are then sewn together to make one block.

Slicing

Dimensions of Mormor's Quilts

	Crib	Full/Queen	King
Finished size	41½″ × 53″	90″ × 108″	110″ × 110″
Size of blocks	11½″	18″	18″
Number of blocks	12	20	25
Number of blocks across	3	4	5
Number of blocks down	4	5	5
Number of triangles	96	160	200
Number of hexagons	48	80	100
Borders, finished size	1″, 2½″	2″, 3″, 4″	2″, 3″, 5″

Fabric Requirements, Mormor's Quilt

	Crib	Full/Queen	King
Background	2 yards	5½ yards	6½ yards
Light	¾ yard	3 yards	3½ yards
Medium	1½ yards	3½ yards	4½ yards
Dark	½ yard	3¼ yards	3½ yards

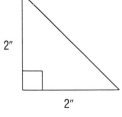

2″

2″

Fig. 14-2

Before you begin you will need to make a pattern for a 2″ × 2″ triangle (Fig. 14-2) out of graph paper or Mylar. If you have plastic pieces for Quilt Block of the Month by Plastics Unlimited, you won't need to make the pattern. Use piece #5.

Crib Size

Note: Crib piece sizes are smaller than full/queen and king. The hexagon piece is 3″ × 6″ and the strips are 1″.

Background (2 yards)
Tear into piece A, 1½ yards (54″), and piece B, ½ yard (18″).
From piece A slice:
    4 pieces outside border 3″ × 54″

4 pieces binding 2″ × 54″
6 pieces 3″ × 54″. Cut these into 48 pieces 3″ × 6″
From piece B slice:
48 squares 3¼″. Cut these in half to make 96 triangles

Light fabric (¾ yard)
Slice (on length) 30 pieces 1″ × 27″

Medium fabric (1½ yards)
Slice 4 pieces inner border 1½″ × 54″
Slice 30 pieces 1″ × 54″

Dark fabric (½ yard)
Slice 25 pieces 1″ × 18″

Full/Queen Size

Background (5½ yards)
Tear into piece A, 3¼ yards (117″), and piece B, 2¼ yards (81″).
From piece A slice:
4 pieces outside border 4½″ × 117″
4 pieces binding 2″ × 117″
4 pieces 4″ × 117″. Cut these into 52 pieces 9″ × 4″
From piece B slice:
4 pieces 4″ × 81″. Cut these into 36 pieces 9″ × 4″
5 pieces 4⅜″ × 81″. Cut these into 90 squares 4⅜″ × 4⅜″

Light fabric (3 yards)
Slice the whole piece into 1½″ strips on the length. You may want
to tear your fabric into two 54″ pieces first to make it easier to cut
and to work with.

Medium fabric (3½ yards)
Tear into piece A, 3 yards (108″), and piece B, ½ yard (18″).
From piece B slice:
28 pieces 1½″ × 18″
From piece A slice:
4 pieces middle border 3½″ × 108″
Slice the remaining portion into 18 pieces 1½″ × 108″

Dark fabric (3¼ yards)
Tear into piece A, 2¾ yards (99″), and piece B, ½ yard (18″)
From piece B slice:
28 pieces 1½″ × 18″
From piece A slice:
4 pieces inner border 2½″ × 99″
Slice the remaining portion into 20 pieces 1½″ × 99″

King Size

Background (6½ yards)
Tear into piece A, 3½ yards (126″), and piece B, 3 yards (108″).
From piece A slice:
4 pieces outer border 5½″ × 126″

4 pieces binding 2″ × 126″
3 pieces 4″ × 126″. Cut these into 42 pieces 9″ × 4″
From piece B slice:
    5 pieces 4″ × 108″. Cut into 60 pieces 9″ × 4″
    5 pieces 4⅜″ × 108″. Cut into 120 squares 4⅜″ × 4⅜″

Light fabric (3½ yards)

Slice the whole piece into 1½″ strips on the length. You may want to tear your fabric into two 63″ (1¾ yards) pieces first.

Medium fabric (4½ yards)

Tear into piece A, 3 yards (108″), and piece B, 1½ yards (54″).
From piece A slice:
    4 pieces middle border 3½″ × 108″
    Slice the remaining portion into 18 pieces 1½″ × 108″
From piece B slice:
    28 pieces 1½″ × 54″ pieces

Dark fabric (3½ yards)

Tear into piece A, 2¾ yards (99″), and piece B, ¾ yard (27″).
From piece A slice:
    4 pieces inner border 2½″ × 99″
    Slice the remaining portion into 1½″ strips (21 pieces 1½″ × 99″).
From piece B slice:
    28 pieces 1½″ × 27″

Piecing

1. Cut pieces 4″ × 9″ (crib 3″ × 6″) from background fabric. Trim off the four corners with the triangle pattern you made (page 122). See the Dimensions of Mormor's Quilts chart for numbers of hexagons needed.

2. All strips are 1½″ wide except crib, which are 1″. Take a strip of light fabric (Strip 1) and lay it right side up on your sewing machine. Place one side of hexagons right side down, leaving ½″ gap between pieces as shown in Fig. 14-3. You will be able to fit ten pieces on each yard of fabric. Stitch hexagons to strip.

3. With sharp scissors, carefully cut apart the units as follows: Lay strip down, as shown in Fig. 14-3. First pull forward the second block, then cut between the first and second block. Pull forward the third block, then cut between the second and third, etc. When you have finished cutting, press seam toward strip.

4. Now, very important, *trim* even with edges, by placing the Quilter's Rule, Jr. on top. A vertical inch mark should be in the seam between the new strip and the block piece. Make a horizontal cut with your rotary cutter.

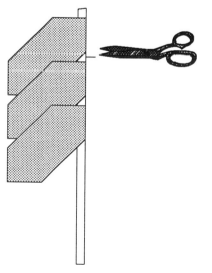

Fig. 14-3

5. Lay another 1½″ strip (crib 1″) of light fabric (Strip 2) on the machine right side up. Place the other edges of the units you have just pieced on this strip as shown in Fig. 14-4, right sides together.

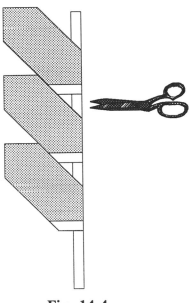

Fig. 14-4

6. After you have sewn the seams, cut apart these units as follows: Pull down the second unit, then cut between the first and second. Pull down the third unit, then cut between the second and third, etc. Press toward the new strip. Trim.

7. Now take a 1½″ strip (crib 1″) of medium fabric (Strip 3) and sew it right sides together to one long edge of your pieced unit as shown in Fig. 14-5. Cut apart units.

8. Sew a medium strip (Strip 4) to the other long edge of your units as well. After pressing, lay the piece right side up to square it off (Fig. 14-6).

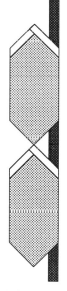

Fig. 14-5

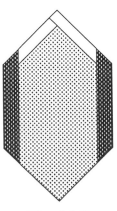

Fig. 14-6

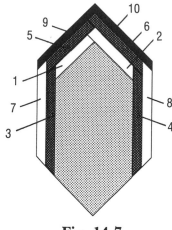

Fig. 14-7

9. Your next strip (Strip 5) is the medium fabric. Position it for sewing and trimming just like Strip 1 (Fig. 14-7).

10. Position Strip 6 (also medium) for sewing and trimming just as you did Strip 2. Strip 7 (light) is sewn and trimmed in the same position as Strip 3. Strip 8 (light) is sewn and trimmed in the same position as Strip 4. Strips 9 and 10 are the dark fabric, which is used only twice. Strip 9 is sewn and trimmed like Strips 5 and 1. Strip 10 is sewn and trimmed like Strips 6 and 2. There are still two edges of the original print left.

11. You will now sew two triangles to each block to make it into a square. *Do not* sew these to the background corner. I have already made that mistake. Sew them to the light fabric sides (Fig. 14-8). The triangles are made from a 4⅜″ square (crib 3¼″). They are, of course, sewn on with a ¼″ seam. It might be easier if you "nub" these triangles by placing the triangle under the 4″ line of the ruler and removing the tips with your rotary cutter. It takes a little time, but pays off later.

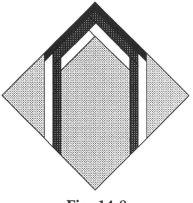

Fig. 14-8

Finishing

Sew squares together in groups of four to make blocks (Fig. 14-9). It will take this many blocks to make rows across:

	Crib	Full/Queen	King
	3	4	5

and rows down:

	Crib	Full/Queen	King
	4	5	5

Fig. 14-9

Sew your dark border first—sides, then top and bottom. The middle border is the medium fabric, followed by the background fabric. (See page 9 for more about borders.)

Now refer to Chapter 1 for information about basting and tying or quilting.

Chapter 15

Little Red
School House

The Little Red School House is not a quilt you naturally think of when you think of quick quilts. It is an old traditional pattern, as are many of the others found in this book. Of the many variations of the School House, we will use one of the most common designs (Fig. 15-1).

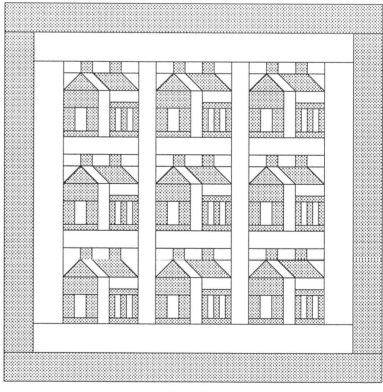

Fig. 15-1

This is not a beginning pattern. I recommend that you make at least one other quilt from this book first. We will piece most of the block by the slice. However, for one row, the roof line, we will use traditional machine-piecing methods.

Accuracy is even more important than usual. Your slices need to match your pattern piecing exactly. There are eight seams across the width of your block. If you are off by $\frac{1}{16}''$ per seam, your block will be off by $\frac{1}{2}''$. This will make your roof line up to $\frac{1}{2}''$ too large or too small. Follow the directions, set your seam guide, and you won't have problems.

Slicing

For this quilt the borders are slightly different. The light fabric is cut one size for sashing between the blocks, larger for outside the blocks and then there is a dark border. An accent border can be placed before the dark border.

Dimensions of Quilts, Little Red School House

	Wall Hanging	Twin	Full	Queen	King
Finished size	40″ × 40″	71″ × 84″	71″ × 105″	95″ × 107″	118″ × 118″
Size of blocks	8″	13″	13″	13″	13″
Total number of blocks	9	12	15	20	36
Number of blocks across	3	3	3	4	6
Number of blocks down	3	4	5	5	6
Borders, finished size	3″, 3″	5″, 5″	5″, 5″	5″, 5″	5″, 5″

Fabric Requirements, Little Red School House

	Wall Hanging	Twin	Full	Queen	King
Light fabric	1¼ yds	3½ yds	4½ yds	5¾ yds	8½ yds
Dark fabric	1¼ yds	4¼ yds	5 yds	5¾ yds	7½ yds

Slicing Information for Little Red School House

Note: Before slicing, you need to tear some yardages as follows: For the twin size, tear your light fabric (3½ yards) into two pieces, 68″ and 58″. Tear dark fabric (4¼ yards) into two pieces, 1½ yards (54 inches) and 2¾ yards (99 inches). For the full size, tear your light fabric (4½ yards) into two pieces, 2½ yards (90 inches) and 2 yards (72 inches).Tear dark fabric (5 yards) into two pieces, 2 yards (72 inches) and 3 yards (108 inches). For the queen size, tear your light and dark fabric (5¾ yards) into two pieces, 3 yards (108 inches) and 2¾ yards (99 inches). For the king size, tear your light fabric (8½ yards) into three pieces: 3½ yards (126 inches), 2½ yards (90 inches), and 2½ yards (90 inches). Tear dark fabric (7½ yards) into three pieces: 3½ yards (126 inches), 2½ yards (90 inches), and 1½ yards (54 inches). Slice all pieces on the *length*.

	Wall Hanging		Twin		Full		Queen		King	
	No. of Slices	Size of Slices	No. of Slices	Size of Slices	No. of Slices	Size of Slices	No. of Slices	Size of Slices	No. of Slices	Size of Slices
Light										
Sashing	4	2½″ × 45″	4	4½″ × 68″	4	4½″ × 90″	4	4½″ × 108″	4	4½″ × 126″
									6	4½″ × 90″
Border	4	3½″ × 45″	2	5½″ × 68″	4	5½″ × 90″	4	5½″ × 108″	4	5½″ × 126″
			2	5½″ × 58″						
Window	2	1¼″ × 45″	2	1½″ × 58″	2	1½″ × 72″	2	1½″ × 99″	4	1½″ × 90″
Door	1	1½″ × 45″	1	2½″ × 58″	1	2½″ × 72″	1	2½″ × 99″	2	2½″ × 90″
Chimney	2	2″ × 22″	3	3½″ × 58″	3	3½″ × 72″	3	3½″ × 99″	3	3½″ × 90″
	1 (center)	3″ × 22″								
Above window	1	1½″ × 36″	2	2½″ × 58″	2	2½″ × 72″	3	2½″ × 99″	6	2½″ × 90″
Between door and windows	2	1¾″ × 45″	2	2½″ × 58″	2	2½″ × 72″	2	2½″ × 99″	4	2½″ × 90″
Dark										
Border	4	3½″ × 45″	4	5½″ × 99″	4	5½″ × 108″	4	5½″ × 108″	4	5½″ × 126″
Binding	4	2″ × 45″	4	2″ × 99″	4	2″ × 108″	4	2″ × 108″	4	2″ × 126″
Window	3	1¼″ × 45″	3	1½″ × 54″	3	1½″ × 72″	3	1½″ × 99″	6	1½″ × 90″
Door	2	1½″ × 45″	2	2½″ × 54″	2	2½″ × 72″	2	2½″ × 99″	4	2½″ × 90″
Chimney	2	1¾″ × 22″	2	2½″ × 54″	2	2½″ × 72″	2	2½″ × 99″	2	2½″ × 90″
Above door	1	2½″ × 45″	2	3½″ × 54″	2	3½″ × 72″	2	3½″ × 99″	4	3½″ × 90″
Above window	2	1½″ × 45″	2	1½″ × 54″	2	1½″ × 72″	2	1½″ × 108″	8	1½″ × 54″
Below door and window	3	1¼″ × 45″	3	1½″ × 54″	3	1½″ × 72″	3	1½″ × 108″	12	1½″ × 54″

Piecing

Now let's begin. Set the seam guide on your machine. If you don't have a seam guide that screws onto your machine, get a magnetic one (Dritz). If you have to use a magnetic guide, measure and place a piece of masking tape on the seam line. Place your magnet guide on the tape line. You will be more aware if you move your guide. The screw-on guides are out there—try and find one. Sewing machine dealers should be able to get one for your machine. If not, contact Quilter's Square, Lexington, Kentucky.

I will take you one little piece at a time as we build this house.

1. For the window unit sew a 1½″ dark to a 1½″ light strip (use 1¼″ strips for wall hanging). Press the seam toward the dark. Sew another dark strip to a light, then sew a dark between the two lights to form the unit shown in Fig. 15-2. (You will need to do this twice for the king size.) Slice this unit into 4½″ slices (wall hanging 3″ slices), so that you have the following number of window units:

Wall Hanging	Twin	Full	Queen	King
9	12	15	20	36

Fig. 15-2

2. For the door unit sew a dark 2½″ strip to a light 2½″ strip (use 1½″ strips for the wall hanging). Press toward dark. Sew a dark to the other side of light. Press toward dark. Slice into 4½″ slices (wall hanging 3″), so that you have the following number of door units (Fig. 15-3).

Wall Hanging	Twin	Full	Queen	King
9	12	15	20	36

3. Take a 3½″ strip of dark (wall hanging 2½″). Lay it on the machine right side up. Place the door slices horizontally, right side down, on this strip. Leave a scant ¼″ space between door

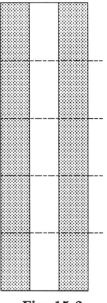

Fig. 15-3

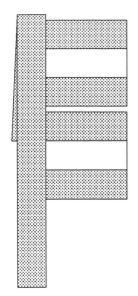

Fig. 15-4

slices placed on the dark strip. Sew down the strip. This attaches the top of the door unit to the area above it.

4. Cut these apart by folding the strip, matching up the edges of the blocks. Cut the strip at the fold (Fig. 15-4). Press toward the strip.

5. Now use a 1½″ strip of dark fabric (1¼″ for wall hanging) for the bottom of the door unit. Lay it on the machine right side up. Place the door slices right side down on this strip. Leave a scant ¼″ space between door slices placed on the dark strip. Sew. Cut apart, as in Step 4 (Fig. 15-5). Press toward 1½″ strip.

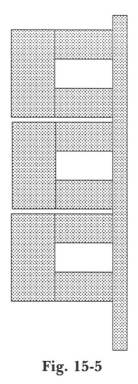

Fig. 15-5

6. Still using 1½″ strips of dark, sew to the top and bottom of window units. (For the wall hanging, the dark strips *above* the window are 1½″ and *below* the window are 1¼″.) Continue to leave a scant ¼″ between blocks (Figs. 15-6, 15-7). We will square it all off in a bit.

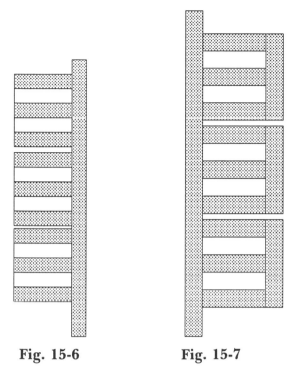

Fig. 15-6   Fig. 15-7

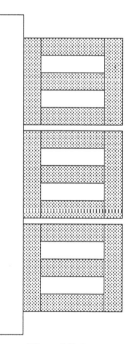

7. Now take a 2½″ strip of light (1½″ strip for wall hanging), sew it on the *top* of window slices, just as you sewed on the dark. Cut apart (Fig. 15-8). Press toward dark.

8. Lay your window unit on the cutting mat. It should be 5½″ (4¼″ wall hanging) wide. Place a large Quilter's Ruler on top. Line the ruler lines up with the internal lines in the piece. Trim off the excess. Turn the piece 180° and trim the other side.

9. Now lay the door unit on the mat. It should be 6½″ wide (3½″ wall hanging). Again, line up your ruler and trim both sides.

10. Sew the left side of the window unit to a light strip. Make sure the light fabric above the window is on top. Cut apart. Press toward new strip. Now join the two sections of the bottom of your house (Fig. 15-9). Sew the door unit to the other side of each light strip/window unit. Press. Now is the time to measure your work. You should have 13½″ across the top by 8½″ up and down (wall hanging 8½″ × 5¾″).

Fig. 15-8

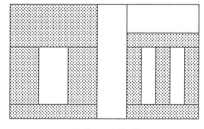

Fig. 15-9

11. Now it's time to make the roof line. But first we'll draw it on graph paper. (I use paper with 8 squares to the inch.) Draw a 3″ by 13″ (wall hanging 1½″ × 8″) rectangle. Measure across the top 3″, 2″, 5″, 3″ (wall hanging 1½″, 1¼″, 3¾″, 1½″). Label each piece as in Fig. 15-10 and add ¼″ seam allowance to the paper. Because the seam allowance lines overlap, it's a good idea to use different-colored pencils to draw the seam allowances.

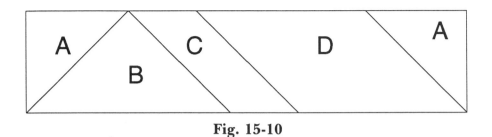

Fig. 15-10

12. To make your templates, cut one pattern piece at a time out of Mylar template material. Lay your Mylar on top of the piece of graph paper. Tape it in place. With a metal edge ruler and a sharp art knife (such as X-acto or Olfa), cut the pattern pieces including the seam allowance. The corner pieces on the right and left (A) are the same. You will need to reverse the template to get the proper angle. At this point I find it helpful to punch a hole at the corners of the finished size of the pattern pieces. I use an ⅛″ hole punch to punch this hole right at the intersection of the seam lines. This will help match them up as they are sewn.

13. Now draw around your templates on the wrong side of the fabric, and cut out. See the note in general instructions on page 16 on using starch. Make sure your piece is placed correctly on the fabric. The right side of your templates should be face down on the wrong side of your fabric. You will be cutting off the line that you draw. You will need the following number of each of these pieces: A (light) pieces; A (light, reversed) pieces; B (dark) pieces; C (light) pieces; and D (dark) pieces:

	Wall Hanging	Twin	Full	Queen	King
	9	12	15	20	36

14. Sew the roof pieces together by matching the seam allowance points (Fig. 15-11). Pay attention to your seam guide. Using straight pins, stab through the intersections. Line them up and sew together. Sew the roof line to lower portion of house (Fig. 15-12). I use my automatic basting stitch to check whether my seams match up before stitching on normal stitch length. Press toward the lower section.

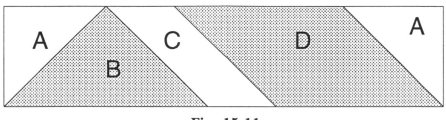

Fig. 15-11

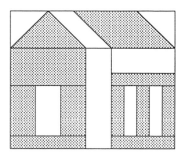

Fig. 15-12

15. Before assembling your chimney unit, measure your roof line. The left chimney must align with the top of piece C. To assemble the chimney row, sew three 3½" light strips to two 2½" dark strips (for wall hanging use 2" light at outside edges, 3" light for the center, and your 1¾" dark strips) to form the unit shown in Fig. 15-13. Press seams toward dark.

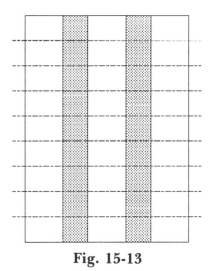

Fig. 15-13

16. Slice into 2½" slices (wall hanging 1¾"). Sew one slice at the top of each roof line (Fig. 15-14). Press toward chimney. Now the hard work is over. The blocks are completed.

17. For the horizontal sashing between bottom edge and chimney, take a strip of light fabric as follows:

Wall Hanging	Twin	Full	Queen	King
2½"×36"	4½"×68"	4½"×90"	4½"×108"	4½"×126"

With your strip right side up and School House blocks right side down, sew the strip to the bottom edge of the following number of School House blocks:

Wall Hanging	Twin	Full	Queen	King
6	9	12	16	30

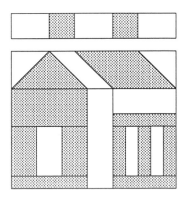

Fig. 15-14

18. Cut apart the blocks and press seam toward the sashing. Square up the blocks.

19. Now lay out and sew into vertical columns. Sew an additional block onto the bottom of each column. Press toward sashing. You need the following number of blocks per column:

	Wall Hanging	Twin	Full	Queen	King
	3	4	5	5	6

Fig. 15-15

20. Lay one column right side down on an inner vertical sashing strip. Stitch, then press toward sashing. To match your columns accurately, draw lightly, on the wrong side of the sashing you just stitched, a line that continues the horizontal seam lines of the blocks. Now sew on the next column, then your other sashing strip(s) (Fig. 15-15).

21. Sew on outside light border strips, sides first, then top and bottom (Fig. 15-16). These outside strips are a little wider than the inner sashing.

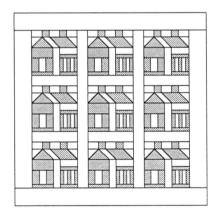

Fig. 15-16

22. Sew on the dark border, sides first, then the top and bottom.

Finishing

Quilting

In traditional Little Red School Houses, the light areas are quilted in a crosshatch pattern. The house is generally outline-quilted. Use a nice cable quilting for the sashing.

Binding

After quilting, use dark binding to finish the piece.

The Little Red School House is complete. You have just finished an heirloom. I have a feeling you won't stop now.

Index

Page numbers in **bold** indicate major projects